The dust had not settled and the dead had not been buried when Israel's propaganda machine went into full swing. They set up a straw man and argued that, "technically speaking," Jenin was not a "massacre." We may never know how many Palestinians died in Jenin. In the end, however, it is not the number who died that will tell the story. It is the savage cruelty experienced by those who survived Israel's assault that will ultimately define the legacy of this devastated square mile of earth. Their story must be told and remembered.

—Dr. James Zogby,
President of the Arab American Institute

Since the beginning of the al-Aqsa Intifada, photojournalist Mahfouz Abu Turk has been beaten and wounded by the Israeli army four times and has been arrested once. After he worked on *Searching Jenin,* the Israeli government revoked Mahfouz's Jerusalem residency for two months, thereby forcing him to make a difficult choice. He could risk imprisonment by remaining in Jerusalem illegally, or he could leave his family, his home, and his job.

Mahfouz Abu Turk was one of the first reporters to enter the Jenin refugee camp. On April 16, Mahfouz and a team of three other journalists approached the camp on foot. They watched the patrolling tanks and waited for an opportunity to enter. Finally, when they thought it was clear, they ran into the camp. Just then an Israeli tank rumbled around the corner and the commander spotted them. In a few moments they were being held at canon-point.

A little later, Mahfouz noticed an opportunity and dodged around a corner. He was making his escape when he ran into more Israelis. They blindfolded him, handcuffed him, and threw him into an Israeli jeep. Then they took him to Salem where he found dozens of Jenin residents in detention. Mahfouz was not allowed to call his family or a lawyer. The Israelis interrogated and harassed Mahfouz for twenty-four hours. His wife and his friends had no idea if he was alive or dead. For that day he was one of the Disappeared of Jenin.

Jenin Refugee Camp

1. Zahrah neighborhood
2. Entrance to Sahah
3. UN Compound
4. Elementary school for girls
5. Martyr's Cemetery
6. Al-Kbir Mosque
7. Jenin Hospital
8. Center of Sahah
9. Abdullah Azam Mosque
10. Al-Ansar Mosque
11. Jurit al-Dahab neighborhood
12. Sumran neighborhood
13. Damaj neighborhood
14. Hawashin neighborhood
15. Al-Jabriat neighborhood

Jenin Street

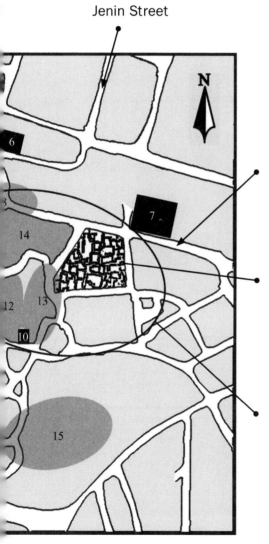

N

Hospital Street

These are outlines of actual
buildings prior to the 2002
invasion. This is representative of the housing density
throughout the Jenin refugee
camp.

The majority of structures in
this area were destroyed or
damaged.

Searching
Jenin

Searching Jenin
is part of the Bridge between the Cultures series.
Other titles include:

The Road from Damascus: A Journey Through Syria
by Scott C. Davis

A Pen of Damascus Steel:
Political Cartoons from an Arab Master
by Ali Farzat

Steel & Silk:
Men and Women Who Shaped Syria 1900-2000
by Sami Moubayed

An Intimate Dinner Party:
Essays by New American Writers
in Arabic and English, Vol. 1
by John Milton Wesley, et al.

Searching Jenin

Eyewitness Accounts
of the
Israeli Invasion 2002

Edited by Ramzy Baroud

Cune

Searching Jenin: Eyewitness Accounts of the Israeli Invasion 2002
Cune Press Seattle 2003
© 2003 Cune Press — All Rights Reserved
(The first US edition is a revision of the first foreign edition)

First US Edition
1 3 5 7 9 8 6 4 2

Edited by Ramzy Baroud. Project Facilitator: Ali Samudi. Assistant Editor:
Suzanne Baroud. All photographs by Mahfouz Abu Turk unless otherwise
noted. Cover and interior Arabic calligraphy is kufic-style Arabic script
arranged in a square shape by Mamoun Sakkal. The square kufic design spells
out *al-kashf an Jenin* or "searching Jenin" in Arabic. Special thanks to editor
Eric Soderlund and proofreader Lorna Burden.

Library of Congress Cataloging-in-Publication Data
Searching Jenin : eyewitness accounts of the Israeli invasion / forward
by Noam Chomsky ; edited by Ramzy Baroud ; photojournalist, Mahfouz Abu
Turk ; project facilitator, Ali Samudi.— 1st ed.
    p. cm.
Includes bibliographical references and index.
  ISBN 1-885942-33-8 (cloth)—ISBN 1-885942-34-6 (pbk.)
  1. Al-Aqsa Intifada, 2000—Casualties—West Bank—Jenin. 2. Al-Aqsa
Intifada, 2000—Personal narratives, Palestinian Arab. 3. Military
occupation. 4. Israel—Military policy. 5. Palestinian Arabs—West
Bank—Jenin—Interviews. I. Baroud, Ramzy. II. Abu Turk, Mahfouz. III.
Title.
  DS119.765 .S43 2003

                    2002015543

Copies of *Searching Jenin* can be purchased from
your local independent bookstore, from www.cunepress.com,
or by calling 1-800-445-8032.

Cune Press, PO Box 31024, Seattle, WA 98103
Ph (206) 782-0136   Fax (206) 782-1330

www.cunepress.com

Searching Jenin is part of the Bridge between the Cultures Series from Cune
Press. (Jesir al-Thaqafat.) For more: www.cunepress.com

We wish to thank the Arab American Community Coalition for its support.

Contents

Preface

Noam Chomsky

Twenty years ago, after an earlier upsurge of settler-IDF violence, one of Israel's most eminent writers, Boaz Evron, wrote a sardonic account of how to deal with the lower orders—the *Araboushim* in Israeli slang. Israel should "keep them on a short leash" so they recognize "that the whip is held over their heads." As long as too many people are not being visibly killed, then Western humanists can "accept it all peacefully," asking, "What is so terrible?"

US-Israeli propagandists understand this lesson without his advice. They made sure—it wasn't very hard—that scrutiny of the vicious crimes in Jenin, Nablus, Ramallah, and elsewhere would focus on one primary question: Was there a purposeful massacre of hundreds of civilians in the Jenin refugee camp? If not, then civilized people can "accept it all peacefully." After all, surely no one but an anti-Iraqi racist would object too strenuously if Iraqi forces commemorated the 35th anniversary of a harsh and brutal military occupation of Israel by rampaging through Israeli cities, levelling large areas with bulldozers and tanks, keeping the population under siege for weeks without food or water or access to medical care, destroying cultural centers and the institutions of government and archaeological treasures in ancient towns, making it crystal clear to the Yids in every possible way that "the whip is held over their heads"—but not slaughtering hundreds of them at once—slowly instead.

The guardians of journalistic integrity also understand this lesson without instruction. Reviewing the handling of "the Jenin story," the most prestigious media "watchdog," the *Columbia Journalism Review*, condemns the British press for "embracing Israel's guilt as established fact" and ridicules the UN for planning an investigation that would obviously be tainted by the "political sympathies" of any "team" it would assemble. But all was not lost: "Enter the independent US news media, on a fact-finding mission of their own," which refuted the anti-Israel slanders and revealed that there was "no deliberate, cold-blooded murder of hundreds." To translate, the "independent US media" reached exactly the same conclusions about mass slaughter as the disreputable British media (and others), which, however, failed the test of "independence" by not adopting the framework of US-Israeli propaganda as rigidly as the editors of the *Review* deem appropriate.

In such ways, the US-backed Israeli war crimes in the spring invasion were transformed into yet another demonstration of the dedication of the US client state to the "purity of arms," yet another proof that it upholds "moral sensitivity [as] a principle of political life" and "is held to a higher law, as interpreted by journalists" (*New York Times*); and that it is guided by "high moral purpose" perhaps unique in history (apart from the US itself) (*Time* magazine). That is an achievement of which any propaganda system should be proud. Fortunately, the "independent US media" did not quite merit the insulting praise of their cheerleader. Careful readers could learn at least a little about the crimes that had taken place, though not in the shocking detail presented in the Israeli and foreign press. And crucially, they were protected carefully from the complicity of their own government. To overcome these barriers to comprehension is a task of utmost importance, if further tragedy is to be averted.

Introduction
Ramzy Baroud

Chaos wrought by Israeli armored vehicles and snipers enforcing a curfew trapped a young Palestinian journalist. Mae Shaheen had entered the camp at dawn and paced the dusty streets for hours. She spent her day meeting people and recording their testimonies. But her interviews took longer than planned. Now the light was growing dim, and she found herself walking alone through abandoned lanes. There were no taxis to carry her back home. Residents who might have helped had sealed their doors. They did not trust knocking strangers. The only sound she could hear was the roar of the tanks' diesel engines in the distance. Everything else was silent.

As she walked, Mae saw a neighborhood in ruins. Where were the men, women, and children who had lived here just days before? Cinder block houses and apartments were smashed. The scene was surreal. It was like a Hollywood production set. By now the sun had set and a desert chill settled in. The electricity was off, street lights were dead. The neighborhood waited in darkness. A curfew had been imposed at dusk, and Mae Shaheen knew that she was in trouble.

Mae could hear the tanks closing in. She could hear the loudspeakers. "Those who violate the curfew will be shot!" they announced in Arabic. Mae found a place in the rubble and hid in fear. In a few minutes the tanks turned and the sound of their engines grew more distant. She could hear single shots, then bursts of fire. The shots were on the other side of the camp. The sound of the tanks grew more distant. Still, Mae waited.

Two hours after midnight, Mae's colleague, Ali Samudi, called Mae on her cell phone, took down directions, then defied the army's orders and stole into the camp. He raced through the abandoned streets in his battered 1988 Fiat, protected only by his velocity. He was able to retrieve Mae, and the two fled to safety outside the camp. The following morning, Mae Shaheen returned to the Jenin refugee camp with a crew of five journalists who carried tape recorders, cameras, and a long list of questions.

Mae's story was typical. The team of Palestinian journalists had close calls, overcame obstacles, and endured hardships while collecting material for *Searching Jenin*. They sought to record a segment of the Arab-Israeli conflict, an event that has become a symbol of the uprising known as the Al-Aqsa Intifada.

The Israeli invasion of Jenin is remembered by Palestinians as a massacre whereas Israelis recall a fair battle. To Israelis Jenin is an example of soldiers fighting "terrorists." The international community can't make up its mind about Jenin. Some accuse Israel of war crimes, while others advocate Israel's "right to defend itself."

Television, radio, and print news outlets presented the opportunity for Israeli soldiers and officers to spread their version of the events in Jenin. Yet the residents of the camp—those witnesses to whatever atrocities occurred, the ones who pitched tents on the ruins of their homes—could not amplify their voices to the same level. *Searching Jenin* documents their perspective. It is the chorus of Jenin's Palestinian refugees. In this book their words bypass the mass media filters, described by Chomsky, that normally would twist or frame their meaning. Their voices dodge the denials and exaggerations of politicians. Their emotions are immune to political sensitivities that ensnarl the United Nations and other international organizations.

When Scott C. Davis of Cune Press approached me about a book on Jenin, I was skeptical—the cards seemed stacked against us. Some warned that it would be impossible to penetrate Jenin, which was under an extremely tight curfew. With the world's attention focused on the region, Israelis would restrict those entering the camp. To add to the difficulty of obtaining interviews, the invasion and the ensuing destruction drove many Jenin residents from their homes and scattered them throughout towns and villages in the West Bank. Most daunting of all, the Israelis were tightening their iron fist around the entire West Bank. It would be a dangerous place for journalists. In truth, it would be nearly impossible for them to gain entry to this war zone.

The start of *Searching Jenin* was anything but promising. I traveled to Jordan and tried for a full month to enter the West Bank. But Israeli officials refused to acknowledge my American citizenship. To them I was a Palestinian—end of story—and they denied permission to enter.

I countered by assembling a team of Palestinian journalists who were already in the West Bank. The team included Mahfouz Abu Turk and Ali Samudi, who were two of the first journalists to enter the Jenin refugee camp in the final days of the Israeli invasion. Abu Turk, a Reuters photojournalist, snapped some of the first photos from Jenin, and Ali Samudi recorded much of the footage aired by Qatar's Al-Jazeera television and other leading news agencies around the world.

Searching Jenin examines the April invasion through the eyes of those who lived it. The book presents a missing link in the drama known by many as the Jenin Massacre and by others simply as the Battle of Jenin. It narrates the story, not by a third party, but by the survivors.

Problems and Solutions

Searching Jenin doesn't answer every question regarding atrocities in the refugee camp. While eyewitnesses openly described their own plight, they did not generalize. Yet this book presents information that can be used to draw larger conclusions. One question that this book *can* help to answer: How did the Israeli army and the Palestinian resistance conduct themselves toward the civilians of Jenin?

A question that this book cannot answer: How many Palestinians were killed in Jenin in the two weeks of fighting, bombardment, and home demolitions? Israel still holds hundreds of Palestinian men from the Jenin refugee camp in its prisons in the West Bank and in Israel. Most of these prisoners are confirmed alive, yet the fate of others remains unknown. There is still rubble to be removed. There are still names to be accounted for and missing to be found. Some fighters reportedly rushed to Jenin to help defend the camp prior to the Israeli invasion in early April 2002. These fighters might be reported missing in Tulkarm and Ramallah, but they actually went missing in Jenin. Because Israeli soldiers vandalized and destroyed Palestinian records in hospitals, schools, and government buildings, this question may never be answered.

Most of the work on this book was done during fierce fighting later in the summer when the IDF had reoccupied Jenin. As problems arose, we found creative solutions. For example, when military curfews put the lives of our reporters in danger and made it unwise for them to move, we recruited reporters based in Jenin. These reporters knew the camp intimately. They could avoid the army and gain quick, safe access to residents' homes.

Our local reporters aided us greatly by earning the trust of Jenin's residents. The residents were more at ease relaying experiences to our reporters, rather than to foreign journalists. We had the opportunity to interview families of Palestinian fighters. These were people who often refused to speak about their lives and loved ones with foreign journalists or even with the Arab media. I am especially proud of interviews with people such as the widow of Mahmud Tawalbe, the Islamic Jihad leader who was recognized (along with Abu Jandal) as the leader of the resistance in the camp. Both Tawalbe and Abu Jandal were killed in the fighting. We also managed to interview the only Palestinian who witnessed Abu Jandal's execution.

Although the testimonies of Jenin residents were translated from Arabic, we minimized edits to preserve the character of the interviews. We aimed to reveal the victims as they were and are—innocent, angry, grieving, proud, spontaneous. Our goal was to uncover the lives and emotion behind the casualty figures. Little Rund al-Shalabi shared her grief and inability to comprehend the Israeli soldiers who broke her toys. We preserved Rafidia al-Jamal's emotions when she described how she lay wounded in the street clutching her dead sister while snipers prevented her from reaching her husband who beckoned from their doorway. We waited patiently as some of the witnesses wept through their stories. We asked little children what they wanted to be when they grew up.

In the end, we gathered scores of interviews. We were forced to discard some that were duplicates and those that were cut too short by circumstances beyond our control.

To rebut claims that the testimonies are exaggerations and lies, we included eyewitness accounts from internationals who visited or sneaked into Jenin just after the Israeli army redeployed to the outskirts of the camp. Americans, Europeans, Israelis journalists, international observers, and aid workers bear witness to the atrocities committed by the Israeli armed forces.

Perceptions

It is not Jenin's size or the number of its inhabitants, but rather the events that unfolded in Jenin that make it significant. According to the United Nations Relief and Works Agency (UNRWA), the camp was established in 1953 within the municipal boundaries of the town of Jenin on 373 *du-nums* of land, roughly one square kilometer. The camp's inhabitants, an estimated 13,000 registered refugees, were expelled from villages that are still visible from the camp. These villages are now located within the so-called Green Line in today's Israel. The camp is in the northern stretch of the West Bank. It fell under Israeli occupation with the rest of the West Bank in 1967. The Jenin refugee camp's status changed in 1995 when it was put under the administrative control of the Palestinian Authority (PA), as dictated by the 1993 Oslo Accords.

The Jenin refugee camp is densely populated. Women, children, and elderly constitute nearly two-thirds of its population. Forty-two percent of the camp residents are under fifteen years of age. Half of the population of the neighboring town of Jenin also consists of refugees who have overflowed from the camp. The population of the camp is generally poor with 307 families registered by UNRWA as "special hardship cases." Since the beginning of the uprising, poverty in the camp has increased with the result that food and water are in short supply during military closures and curfews.

We asked a young man about Israel's perception of the impoverished camp. "Israel calls us the house of bees, but we think of our camp as the home of resistance," he said. In fact, for quite some time Israel has considered the Jenin refugee camp a place where "terrorists" thrive. The contrast between Israel's perception of the camp and the perceptions of the camp's residents shaped events. Another factor was the history of interaction between Jenin and Israel since 1967. The Israeli invasion of Jenin is not an isolated effort to tame "bees" or crack down on "terrorists."

When Palestinians staged an uprising against the Israeli military occupation of the West Bank and Gaza in September 2000, Jenin was at the forefront. The residents of the camp suffered many casualties. Israel often claims that fighters from Jenin were leaders in suicide bombings and attacks on Israeli soldiers, armed settlers, and civilians. To understand the invasion of Jenin requires a look at certain events that occurred before the invasion.

The Violence that Preceded

The year 2002 began with violence as Israeli Prime Minister Ariel Sharon promised new tactics to crush Palestinian resistance. When Israel declared its intention to pull out of parts of the West Bank that had been reoccupied after the outbreak of the Intifada, Palestinians were skeptical. They viewed the Israeli move as propaganda designed to improve Israel's image. The Israeli army actually did order the redeployment of its forces on several occasions, yet the Israelis remained too close for Palestinian comfort.

By the beginning of 2002, Israeli tanks were only 100 meters from the Palestinian Authority's headquarters in the West Bank city of Ramallah. Israel continued its deadly raids and assassinations, its incursions into West Bank and Gaza towns, and continued to demolish Palestinian homes—homes and apartment buildings that housed relatives of accused Palestinian fighters. Attacks by Palestinians on Israeli targets increased and claimed the lives of many civilians and soldiers. On January 10, Israeli bulldozers and tanks invaded the Rafah refugee camp in Gaza, demolishing dozens of homes and displacing hundreds. Israel claimed that Palestinian fighters used these homes to target a nearby Jewish settlement built on Palestinian land in the southern Gaza Strip. Less than one week later, a top leader in the Palestinian Fatah movement, Raed al-Karmi, was assassinated by Israeli forces. This act provoked a suicide bomb attack on Israeli civilians in the West Bank town of Hadera, north of Israel. Six people were killed.

Israel retaliated by bombing Tulkarm in the West Bank, killing one and wounding forty. Two days later, on January 21, Israel invaded Tulkarm and, on January 24, Israeli forces assassinated top Hamas leader, Bakr Hamdan, as well as two other Hamas members. Repeating a pattern established after Israel's assassination of al-Karmi, a suicide bomber retaliated one day later and wounded twenty-five Israelis in Tel Aviv. On February 4, Israel killed five Palestinians in Gaza and, on February 19, killed eight Palestinians with missiles and bombs.

At this point Palestinian and Arab media discussed a change of tactics by the Palestinian resistance. The Palestinian Authority and other militant groups were in conflict. Whereas the PA condemned suicide bombings, other groups argued that a suicide bomb is one of the few weapons capable of inflicting painful blows on an enemy that has far superior weapons and much more money. On February 22 and March 3, Palestinian fighters targeted the Israeli military. In the first attack they killed six occupation soldiers and on March 3 they killed seven soldiers. Israel responded to these attacks by bombing Palestinian areas. They killed thirty-three Palestinians, most of whom were civilians, including five children.

Israel's deadly raids and Palestinian bombings increased rapidly. Hundreds were killed and wounded during the month of March 2002. On March 8 alone, Israeli troops killed forty Palestinians in assaults on the West Bank and Gaza. On March 12, thirty-one more Palestinians were killed in Israeli attacks. Palestinian attacks on Israeli troops, settlers, and suicide bombings subsequently increased. On March 27, a suicide bomber killed himself along with nineteen Israelis in Natanya.

On the Political Front

In the weeks before the Jenin invasion, the political front was equally heated. In Israel, a poll conducted by the Israeli daily *Yedioth Ahronoth* revealed that sixty-one percent of the Israeli public was dissatisfied with Sharon's performance. After all, Sharon had not fulfilled his promise of improved security. The Israeli government in turn blamed Yasser Arafat for the escalation of violence, and trapped him in his Ramallah headquarters.

In February 2002, growing interest in a Saudi peace proposal dominated the political arena in the Middle East and also grabbed the attention of Washington. The Saudis formally unveiled their proposal at the Arab Summit in Beirut at the end of March. The proposal promised Israel peace, security, and normal relations in exchange for a full withdrawal from the land Israel had occupied since 1967, the establishment of a Palestinian state with East Jerusalem as its capital, and a fair solution to the problem of over five million Palestinian refugees. The "fair solution" for the refugees signaled a change in Arabs' attitude toward the Palestinian refugees' right of return in accordance with international law. In the past, Arab countries interpreted UN Resolution 194 as a guarantee of the refugees' right to return. This was a major obstacle in previous peace proposals. Although the right to return had been removed, Israel did not embrace the proposal. Israeli officials dismissed the Saudi plan, with some Israelis labeling it a death sentence for the Jewish state. The Israeli rejection eventually influenced Washington's position. US President George W. Bush originally endorsed the Saudi plan but soon stopped using it as a frame of reference and eventually dropped it altogether.

At this time international pressure was pushing Israel to release Arafat from his besieged headquarters in order to attend the Beirut conference. Only one day before the Beirut summit was to begin, Arafat announced that he could not attend because Sharon had put forth new conditions. Sharon had stipulated that any attack against Israeli targets while Arafat was in Beirut would lead to the permanent exile of the Palestinian leader. Both Israel and Arafat knew it was impossible to guarantee that all factions in the Palestinian resistance would adhere to this condition. Not only was the Saudi proposal rejected by Israel, but the way that Israel handled the matter compelled Arab states, including those who are considered moderate, to conclude that Israel was not interested in political dialogue.

According to most accounts, the Israeli offensive began in the Jenin refugee camp in the early hours of Wednesday, April 3. The Israeli army, in its sweep of the West Bank, justified the invasion as an attempt to crack down on Palestinian militants whom Israel accused of masterminding suicide bombings. Media attention remained focused on the Israeli warplanes, armored vehicles, and infantry that had launched an attack on Bethlehem one day earlier. The Israeli attack on Bethlehem and the occupation army's large-scale assault on the West Bank had been denounced by the Vatican, and compelled Egypt to downgrade its diplomatic ties with Israel.

In Jenin, however, Israeli actions were not as visible. The Israeli army imposed a tight siege that isolated the camp and city and dampened news coverage. The Israeli army then destroyed the camp's generators. Most of the events in Jenin were not revealed until after the Israeli army's operation concluded and the curfew was lifted.

Classifying Jenin

War crimes are generally understood to include genocide, crimes against humanity, and mistreatment of civilians or combatants during war. Article 147 of the Fourth Geneva Convention gives the following definition of war crimes:

> Willful killing, torture or inhumane treatment, including
> . . . willfully causing great suffering or serious injury to
> body or health, unlawful deportation or transfer or unlawful
> confinement of a protected person, compelling a protected

person to serve in the forces of a hostile power, or willfully depriving a protected person of the rights of fair and regular trial . . . taking of hostages and extensive destruction and appropriation of property, not justified by military necessity and carried out unlawfully and wantonly.

International lawyers consider the Geneva Conventions as the essential text to be used in defining war crimes. However, the Statutes of the International Criminal Tribunal in The Hague (ICTY) are also an important reference and have governed cases relating to the former Yugoslavia. The Statutes of The Hague indicate that the court has the right to try suspects who have allegedly violated the laws or customs of war. These violations include:

Wanton destruction of cities, towns or villages, or devastation not justified by military necessity; attack, or bombardment, by whatever means of undefended towns, villages, dwellings or buildings; seizure of, destruction or willful damage done to institutions dedicated to religion, charity and education, the arts and sciences, historic monuments, and works of art and science; plunder of public or private property.

Examples of crimes against humanity provided by the tribunal and categorized as crimes committed in armed conflict but directed against civilian populations include: murder, deportation, imprisonment, persecutions on political, racial, and religious grounds.

Amnesty International and Human Rights Watch argue that there is little doubt that many of the acts carried out by the Israeli army in the Jenin refugee camp qualify as war crimes. Not only did the army leave compelling evidence behind, further proof can be found in scores of eyewitness accounts relayed by international observers and journalists, as well as by a few Israeli soldiers.

On May 31, The Israel newspaper *Yedioth Ahronoth* published an interview with Israeli army D-9 bulldozer operator, Moshe Nissim, nicknamed "Kurdi Bear." Nissim's comments were one of a very few accounts that undercut the Israeli government's denial of war crimes. Here is some of what Kurdi Bear had to say:

Many people were inside [the] houses we started to demolish. They would come out of the houses we were working on. I didn't see, with my own eyes, people dying under the blade of the D-9. And I didn't see houses falling down on live people. But if there were any, I wouldn't care at all. I am sure people died inside these houses, but it was difficult to see, there was lots of dust everywhere, and we worked a lot at night. I found joy with every house that came down, because I knew they didn't mind dying, but they cared for their homes. If you knocked down a house, you bury 40 or 50 people for generations. If I am sorry for anything, it is for not tearing the whole camp down.

The Israeli newspaper that quoted Nissim also reported that the young man was dubbed "Bear" by his fellow soldiers because of the forceful way he toppled Palestinian homes. Bear also criticized rights groups:

All the human rights organizations and the UN that messed with Jenin, and turned what we have done there into such an issue, are just bullshitting—lying.

Bear also shared his perception of justice:

I say if a man has done nothing, don't touch him. A man who has done something, hang him, as far as I am concerned. Even a pregnant woman—shoot her without mercy, if she has a terrorist behind her. This is the way I thought in Jenin. I answered to no one. I didn't give a damn. The main thing was to help our soldiers. If I had been given three weeks, I would have had more fun. That is, if they would let me tear the whole camp down. I have no mercy.

Kurdi Bear concludes with a sarcastic comment. "As far as I am concerned," he said, "I left them with a football stadium, so that they can play." It was not, however, an individual man's action that stirred the horror felt by most of those who we interviewed in the camp. Bear stated, "No one [in the Israeli army] expressed any reservations against doing it." The man was not only obeying orders, but he also enjoyed his work. He was good at it. According to Bear, some of the other bulldozer "operators cracked up and needed rest, but I refused to leave, I needed more . . . I had lots of satisfaction in Jenin, lots of satisfaction. It was like getting all the eighteen years of doing nothing into three days. The soldiers came up to me and said, 'Kurdi, thanks a lot. Thanks a lot.'"

Unanswered Questions

How many Palestinians were killed during the Israeli invasion of Jenin? As *Searching Jenin* goes to press, this question cannot be answered because hundreds of men are still detained by the Israeli army. It is impossible to determine how many of the missing are alive and how many are dead. Some international observers have aired their suspicions that the Israeli army transported the bodies of Jenin victims out of the refugee camp for secret burial in the Jordan valley or another remote location. Israeli officials counter that journalists were kept out of the camp after the fighting was over so that Israeli troops could remove booby traps, unexploded shells, and other hazards that might harm the journalists.

The official death toll stands at sixty-three, nearly half of whom have been identified as civilians. In addition, three bodies are unidentifiable and several more are missing. Forensic experts claim that the nature of some wounds indicates that the victims were executed. Others were shot at close range. Eyewitnesses saw Israeli snipers shoot and kill people through the windows of their homes. Others died in their homes when Israeli bulldozers toppled these dwellings. The initial estimates of the death toll (supplied by Palestinian and international humanitarian aid organizations) were much higher than the deaths that have been confirmed to date. Israeli officials accused human rights groups and Palestinians of lying, yet the same tendency for an initial over count has occurred in other disasters including the World Trade Center attacks.

It was Israelis themselves who gave the first indications of a massacre. The *Jerusalem Post* reported that, "behind closed doors," Israeli foreign minister Shimon Peres termed the Israeli army's conduct in the Jenin refugee camp a massacre.

Top Israeli army and government officials estimated deaths in the hundreds, but claimed that most of those killed were "terrorists," not civilians. Israeli army chief spokesman, Brigadier-General Ron Kitery told army radio that "there were apparently hundreds of dead" Palestinians in the camp. These claims make one wonder how much

Israeli officials really knew and why they later reduced the numbers dramatically. Ironically Peres became one of the most vicious opponents of a UN fact-finding mission to Jenin. At its inception, Israel publicly welcomed the fact-finding mission. After negotiations with the UN Security Council, however, Israel refused to allow the UN team to investigate, and Kofi Annan announced that the fact-finding mission had collapsed. The Israeli army claimed to have killed hundreds, yet accused those who cited the same numbers of spreading propaganda.

Who was a fighter and who was a civilian? The vast majority of those living in the Jenin refugee camp are poor civilians who, like most Palestinians, believe a fair solution is an end to the Israeli military occupation. The desire to "destroy Israel" was hardly a common denominator among the witnesses we spoke with—including the families of Palestinian fighters and suicide bombers. Nevertheless, most of the residents strongly supported and continue to support the resistance, because for them the resistance was and is their best hope for protection. This sentiment is apparent in many of the testimonies.

The Jenin residents we interviewed felt that Jenin's fighters had no choice but to engage the advancing Israeli soldiers. They regarded the defense of their refugee camp as a right—not a crime. The Jenin camp residents had prior experience with the Israeli army. The camp had been raided twice in the month and a half preceding the April invasion. In these raids, civilians constituted a large portion of those killed.

In the first days of April, when word spread that the Israeli army was closing in on the camp, it was only natural that those capable of defending their community would do so. Most of the resistance fighters were residents of the camp. However, a few lived in nearby towns and villages. The witnesses testifying in this book referred to the fighters with pride and admiration. They called them the *shebab*, meaning roughly "our boys" in English. Some residents shared their food with the *shebab*, and others prayed for their safety. To many residents, the fighters were the only ones who protected the camp while the international community did nothing—even though the UN is legally responsible for the Jenin camp and the welfare of its residents. Several witnesses describe *shebab* members rescuing families from collapsing or burning homes. In one case, the fighters crawled through a broken window and led the entire family to safety as a bulldozer was demolishing their home.

International law clearly dictates the treatment of combatants in times of war. Although international law prohibits the mistreatment of fighters once apprehended, several witnesses reported seeing Israelis execute captured Palestinian fighters. Some bodies were found with blindfolds and handcuffs. They showed signs of having been shot at close range. The witnesses in this book outlined the dilemma of the *shebab*. The resisters quickly saw that the Israeli army intended to kill them, in action or in handcuffs. What option did that leave them except to fight? And if the fighters had fled, would the United Nations have sent a multinational force to protect Jenin residents?

It is an open question whether the Israeli army bore down harder on Jenin civilians because of the armed resistance than they would have if there had been no resistance at all. The Israeli army maintained that its conduct in the refugee camp was solely aimed at "uprooting the terrorist infrastructure" and was designed to minimize civilian casualties. For their part, Jenin residents saw the *shebab* as protectors whose small arms fire in response to tanks, bulldozers, and armored personnel carriers prevented greater losses. Their judgement is based on memory of Israeli massacres—sometimes against utterly passive Palestinian civilians—going back to the 1940s. A fairly recent example was the massacre in the Sabra and Shatila refugee camps in Beirut in September 1982. In these two enclaves, Lebanese Phalangists butchered approximately 2,200 civilians in less than three days as the Israeli army watched from their guard towers and checkpoints at the perimeters of the camps. The Phalangists were subordinate to Ariel Sharon, who at the time was the Israeli Defense Minister. Jenin residents were familiar with Sharon's brutal tactics. Their interpretation of past experience told them that it was safer to resist.

"What did the world expect us to do? Should we have just laid down peacefully and been crushed under the treads of Israeli tanks? Should we have let the fire engulf our children and should we have scolded them if they screamed?" asked a resident of Jenin.

The Israeli government denies a massacre because it is unlikely that the confirmed death count will reach the original estimate of 500. Regarding the magnitude of the death toll, one has to ask, how many refugees must be killed in order for the Israeli attack on Jenin to be categorized as a massacre?

Following the September 11 terrorist attacks in the United States, estimates of the deaths in the World Trade Center towers reached tens of thousands. Actually, fewer than three thousand died in New York on that dreadful day. What difference does this make? Is the tragedy any less appalling? Does the pain that these individuals experienced deserve less sympathy? Are the killers blamed less for their actions? Is the world less outraged by the catastrophe?

Palestinians and pro-Palestinian activists claim that indeed there was a massacre. They cite fighters handcuffed and shot point blank. According to Amnesty International and Human Rights Watch, evidence supports the claims of war crimes. They cite murder, executions, demolition of homes, the use of human shields, beating and abuse, random shelling, and bombardment of civilian areas.

The Jenin refugee camp is a focal point in the Israeli-Palestinian conflict. The plight of this small camp with its impoverished refugees is representative of Israeli occupation and of Palestinian resistance. It reflects the victimization of the Palestinian people and also demonstrates their determination to use armed struggle to defy occupation. It also exemplifies Israel's unwavering support of its army's conduct in the occupied territories. Colonel "Didi" directed the invasion of Jenin:

> We think there are eighty to one hundred bodies [in Jenin], most if not all of them terrorists. Many of the fatalities among our soldiers were because we behaved as the most moral army in the world and the most careful army in the world.

Israeli radio gave Colonel Didi the opportunity to defend the actions of his soldiers in Jenin. *Searching Jenin* gives people of the camp the opportunity to reply. These testimonies recount Palestinian losses. Yet they also remind the world that the Palestinian voice has not been silenced and continues to long for freedom.

Timeline

Before the Invasion
JANUARY 3, 2002

Israel announces a pull-out from recently reoccupied parts of the West Bank, yet Israeli tanks remain stationed within one hundred meters of the Palestinian Authority's headquarters in Ramallah.

JANUARY 5

Israel claims it discovered a Palestinian ship with fifty tons of light arms and anti-tank missiles on its way to the Palestinian territories via the Red Sea and accuses the Palestinian Authority (PA) of plotting to destroy Israel.

JANUARY 9

Hamas fighters attack Israeli soldiers near the Gaza Strip, kill four.

JANUARY 10

Israeli army bulldozers destroy thirty-two homes of Palestinian refugees in Rafah, leaving hundreds homeless.

JANUARY 15

Israel assassinates top Fatah activist Raed al-Karmi. A leader of Al-Aqsa Brigades vows to retaliate.

JANUARY 17

A member of Al-Aqsa Brigades shoots and kills six Israelis in the Israeli town of Hadera.

JANUARY 18

Israeli warplanes kill one Palestinian and wound forty in an attack on Tulkarm, destroying the PA police headquarters in this West Bank town.

JANUARY 21

Israel invades Tulkarm for the first time since the eruption of the Palestinian uprising in September 2000.

JANUARY 24

The Israeli army assassinates a senior Hamas commander, Bakr Hamdan. Hamas vows retaliation.

JANUARY 27

The first Palestinian woman suicide bomber detonates herself in Jerusalem, killing one Israeli and wounding one hundred.

FEBRUARY 1

Israeli Prime Minister Sharon tells Israeli newspaper *Maariv* that he regrets not killing Arafat twenty years earlier during the Israeli invasion of Lebanon.

FEBRUARY 4

Five Palestinian activists are assassinated by Israel in Gaza.

FEBRUARY 13

Israeli carries out the most extensive attack to date on Gaza.

FEBRUARY 19

Eight Palestinians are killed in an Israeli missile strike. Six Israeli soldiers are killed when Palestinian fighters raid a military checkpoint near Ramallah.

FEBRUARY 20

Sharon promises a "different course of action" to deal with the Intifada.

FEBRUARY 24

Israel allows Arafat to travel to Ramallah.

March 2

A suicide bomber kills eight Israelis, including six children, in an ultra-orthodox neighborhood in Jerusalem.

March 3

Ten Israelis, including seven soldiers, are shot dead by a Palestinian fighter in the West Bank.

March 4

Seventeen Palestinians, including five children, are killed in Ramallah by the Israeli army.

March 5-7

Ten Palestinians and five Israelis are killed in bloody attacks.

March 8

Israeli troops kill forty Palestinians in an assault on the West Bank and Gaza. This is the deadliest day since the outbreak of the Intifada.

March 11

A suicide bomber detonates himself, killing eleven Israelis in a crowded café in Jerusalem.

March 12

The IDF kills thirty-one Palestinians in the West Bank and Gaza and invades Ramallah in the West Bank and refugee camps in Gaza.

March 20

A suicide bomber detonates himself in Galilee, killing seven Israelis.

March 27

The Arab summit in Lebanon opens without the presence of PA President Yasser Arafat. A suicide bomber detonates himself in Netanya killing nineteen Israelis.

March 28

The Arab summit offers Israel peace, security, and normalization in exchange for withdrawal from the occupied territories.

MARCH 29

The Israeli army stages a large-scale attack on Arafat's headquarters in Ramallah. Arafat vows to die rather than to surrender. He also reaffirms his support for the Arab peace proposal.

MARCH 30

US President George Bush urges Arafat, confined to the basement of his headquarters in Ramallah, to do more to crack down on terrorism.

MARCH 31

The Israeli army invades Qalqiliya in the West Bank. A suicide bomb kills sixteen Israelis in Haifa.

APRIL 2

The Israeli army launches a large-scale attack on the West Bank town of Bethlehem by bombing Palestinian targets around the Square and the Church of the Nativity.

Around 7 PM, Israeli tanks move to areas adjacent to Jenin, concentrating mostly in Arabeh and Salem. Hundreds of Israeli troops are deployed to areas near the refugee camp.

The Invasion

APRIL 3

Around 2 AM Israeli tanks begin heavy and systematic shelling of the Jenin refugee camp from all fronts except the east. Israeli troops close in and special forces begin to penetrate the refugee camp and position themselves on the roofs of homes and high buildings, including mosques.

APRIL 4

The Israeli bombardment continues. The Israeli army blocks access to the camp. Special forces continue to locate and capture strategic positions. Units consisting of twenty-five to thirty soldiers take over homes located at the edges of the camp.

APRIL 5

Apache and Cobra helicopters begin heavy bombardment of the Jenin refugee camp, shooting at homes, attempting to provide safe access for tanks and troops. The Israeli army closes the camp from all directions. Access in or out is denied.

APRIL 6 AND 7
Israeli tanks and warplanes bombard the camp in concert. Missiles strike dozens of homes, and shells fall in the center of the camp. Many residents and fighters are killed or hurt, but are denied access to medical facilities.

APRIL 8
The resistance calms down. Israeli troops begin moving from the eastern side of the camp toward the Hawashin neighborhood at the camp's center.

APRIL 9, 10, 11
Thirteen Israeli soldiers are killed in a Jenin battle. The Israeli army begins demolishing homes—often without warning the residents inside. Using giant bulldozers, the Israeli army destroys most of the Damaj and Hawashin neighborhoods, and most of the center of the camp known as the Sahah. Hundreds of homes are leveled and thousands of the camp's residents are expelled to nearby villages or are arrested. Hundreds of residents are forced at gunpoint to leave the camp and go to the town of Jenin.

In conversation behind closed doors, Israeli Foreign Minister Shimon Peres reportedly terms the Israeli army's operations in the Jenin refugee camp a massacre.

APRIL 12
The Israeli army continues its bombardment of the camp. Israel continues to prevent access to the camp, and news surfaces that the army is concealing evidence of an atrocity. Residents who managed to escape the camp speak of a massacre and describe decomposed bodies left in the streets for days.

APRIL 13, 14
The Israeli army limits access by recovery and aid workers. The Israeli High Court permits Red Crescent-Red Cross ambulances to enter the camp, however, the army restricts their movement until it is dark.

APRIL 15

The Red Crescent decides to stop its recovery efforts for lack of cooperation from the Israel army—specifically because of limits placed on the number of aid workers allowed in. The international rights group LAW and the Israeli-based rights group Adalah petition the Israeli Supreme Court to create rescue procedures that will be honored by the Israeli army.

Post Invasion
APRIL 16

In Geneva, a spokesman for United Nations Relief and Works Agency (UNRWA) warns about increasing risk of a human catastrophe. He says that thousands of people in the camp have gone without food or water for days.

APRIL 17

Derrick Pounder, a professor of forensic medicine at Dundee University who is working with Amnesty International, visits the camp and the Jenin Hospital. He conducts an autopsy at the Jenin hospital of a thirty-eight-year-old Palestinian, and concludes that the nature of the killing was "highly suspicious." He says that claims of large numbers of casualties are highly credible.

APRIL 18

Peter Hansen of UNRWA says, "I and my colleagues, working in crisis situations for decades, do not recall a situation where cooperation from the authorities has been less than what we have experienced from the Israeli government."

UN Special Envoy, Terje Larsen tours the ruins of the Jenin camp. He says that Israel's denial of access to the camp is "morally repugnant." He describes the conditions of the camp as "horrific beyond belief."

A spokesman for the Israeli government, Avi Pazner, conveys Israel's rejection of a call by UN Secretary General Kofi Annan to deploy an armed multinational force to the occupied Palestinian territories. He says, "In the present situation, we don't believe that an international presence could be useful."

APRIL 19

US President George Bush's spokesman Ari Fleischer says, "The President has called for the United Nations and the Red Cross to be permitted to have unhindered access to Jenin."

Israeli Foreign Minister Shimon Peres invites Annan to launch a fact-finding mission to the Jenin offensive.

APRIL 20

The United Nations Security Council adopts resolution 1405 to send a fact-finding mission to the Jenin camp.

APRIL 22

Annan appoints a three-member fact-finding team to probe Israel's military assault on the camp.

The Red Cross accuses Israel of breaching the Geneva Conventions by recklessly endangering civilian lives and property during its assault on Jenin. Rene Kosirnik of the Red Cross says, "When we are confronted with the extent of the destruction in an area of civilian concentration, it's difficult to accept that international humanitarian law has been respected."

An Israeli army spokesman, Lieutenant Colonel Olivier Rafowics, accuses the Red Cross of pro-Palestinian bias.

APRIL 23

Heeding an Israeli request, Annan agrees to delay the fact-finding mission until he meets with Israeli envoys at the UN. Shimon Peres says, "We want assurances that the testimonies of Israelis cannot be used against them."

APRIL 28

The Israeli government holds a meeting and decides to block the UN fact-finding mission to Jenin.

APRIL 30

A top UN diplomat, Undersecretary-General Kieran Prendegast, says Annan is considering abandoning the UN mission to Jenin.

MAY 1

Annan announces that the UN fact-finding mission has collapsed.

MAY 3

US-based Human Rights Watch (HRW) publishes a report on the Jenin atrocities that says it has found *prima facie* evidence that the Israeli army committed war crimes in the camp. It calls for a criminal investigation of those responsible.

MAY 4

An overwhelming majority of countries debating at the UN Security Council condemn Israel for rejecting the UN fact-finding mission. The US envoy says Israel's decision was "regrettable" but claims, "There is no evidence of any massacres."

MAY 7

The UN General Assembly adopts a resolution requesting the Secretary-General to present a report "drawing upon the available resources and information on the recent events that took place in Jenin and other Palestinian cities."

AUGUST 1

Annan produces a report that blames both sides for the Jenin casualties. "Combatants on both sides conducted themselves in ways that, at times, placed civilians in harm's way." Israel embraces the report's findings.

AUGUST 2

Human Rights Watch criticizes Annan's report. Peter Bouckaert of HRW says, "Israeli forces committed serious violations of international humanitarian law, some amounting to *prima facie* of war crimes. It is not a report that the United Nations can be proud of."

TESTIMONIES

JENIN RESIDENTS

Tayseer Damaj

Tayseer Muhammad Mahmud Damaj (40) is a gentle man with a dark complexion and a sharp nose. He speaks with boldness and no hesitance. However there is a tone of guilt that can be detected in his voice, and he says he mourns not being able to save loved ones who perished during the attack. Since the Israeli invasion, he complains that he has been moody and very anxious. Tayseer has been unemployed for the last two years.

The Israeli attack on the camp started around three in the morning. We woke up to the sound of explosions beside our home. Our home is located on a hill beside the Damaj neighborhood. My wife and her sister Fadwa al-Jamal were awake. They were scared so they washed themselves and prayed. They did not know what to make of the explosions. Things calmed down and there was some quiet, so I tried to get some sleep. During the time that I was asleep, my wife and her sister stepped outside the house—only about six or seven meters. Because my sister-in-law is a nurse, when Israel attacks she has orders to go directly to the hospital to attend to the wounded. My wife was walking with her to the hospital. I had no idea that they had left. The *shebab* were taking positions to defend the camp. The *shebab* saw my wife and sister-in-law and asked why they came out into the danger.

At that particular moment, the Israelis began firing into the camp again. I was still asleep. Yet I woke up abruptly and stood by the window that opens to the area in front of the house. I heard my wife screaming, "Ambulance! Ambulance!" I started running toward her, crying, "What happened?" Then I ran back into the house and called the ambulance. The relief workers were afraid to come at first. They said Israelis were wounding and killing medical personnel, but eventually they said that they would come. I was still worried that they would not make it. I decided to go out and help my wife, in spite of the heavy firing in the area. I opened the door. I saw my wife lying on her back, and her sister was sitting hunched over on the ground. I cried out to my wife, "What happened to you?" She said, "We have been wounded . . ." and then her words faded. I looked upon my sister-in-law and screamed, "Fadwa, Fadwa!" She groaned, but I could not understand what she was trying to say.

My wife, who was lying on her back, cried out to me, "Fadwa just tried to utter her last supplication to God, but she could not." At that moment, Fadwa died.

I tried to step outside of the house to pull my wounded wife in. I could see that she was bleeding badly. I barely stepped three meters out the door and the soldiers fired at me. I ran back in again and tried to see where the Israelis were positioned so that I could avoid them. I screamed to my wife, asking her to try and crawl toward me just a little bit so that I could reach her. Some of the *shebab* also tried to approach her to pull her to safety, but she shouted at them, "For God's sake, go back! If you come they will kill you!" I tried two or three times to get to her, but it was very difficult.

Tayseer grabs a cigarette and looks at a framed picture of his wife and her sister, then continues.

I felt like I was giving up. I stood by the door and I said, "God, I am leaving this matter in your hands, there is nothing I can do." This whole event took place in five or six minutes. If she would have crawled only two or three meters toward me, I might have been able to do something. I felt that those five minutes were five hours.

Tayseer Muhammad Mahmud Damaj

I went inside to check on our children. We have five children. My oldest daughter is thirteen years old and my youngest is three. I also have a six-year-old, a ten-year-old and an eleven-year-old. They were crying and screaming, so I tried to comfort them. I told my oldest daughter to make sure that none of her sisters and brothers would

48

leave the house. I gave her a candle. I told her to light the candle so that her sisters and brothers would not be afraid. I went toward the door again, doing nothing but cursing this tragic fate. What could I do? My wife was in so much danger, but if I was killed too, who would be there for my children?

Then my wife tried to move. She told me that her leg was very heavy, yet she managed to crawl at least one meter. At that time, the shooting was not as severe, and I managed to get to her. I pulled her all the way up to the door. I thought that maybe the soldiers moved on to another area, so I went back to get Fadwa. But once I got back to the door, two shots were fired at me, and a hand grenade flew right past me. I ran back into the house and closed the door. I hid behind a wall just as a hand grenade exploded. Despite the damage it created, I thought to myself, "at least I know where the soldiers are." I felt, however, I had no hope of reaching Fadwa, because it seemed that the soldiers were based on the top of the mosque. I wasn't sure of that until days later when the Imam of the mosque told me how the Israelis stormed the mosque and took position there.

I went back to my wife. I found a blanket and I moved her onto it. She was bleeding very hard and it was raining. She was muttering things I did not understand. I ran back inside the house. I told the children to make wet towels. What else could I have done? I don't have any medical background and I don't know how to treat a wound. She had a severe wound, nearly 20 centimeters long, around her waist. She was also wounded in the chest and had a broken leg. I could do nothing but proclaim, "There is no God but Allah." I thought, "if the ambulance does not come right away, I will lose my beloved wife." I ran back inside the house, I did not want the children to see their mother dying.

At that moment I heard a siren. I knew it was the ambulance and went running out of the house like a madman. It was completely dark because the hand grenade they threw from the top of the mosque cut out the electricity. I stood in the street and started screaming, "Here, here!" My neighbors came out too. They bravely helped me carry my wife, as if there were no soldiers and no shooting. The ambulance finally got to us. They wanted to put my wife inside, but I refused to let them move her without a stretcher. I was afraid that her leg would cause terrible pain if they carried her without a stretcher, but they told me they were all out of stretchers.

"At least tie her broken leg to a splint!" I said. But they told me that there was no time. Then I said good bye to her. "I cannot come with you," I explained, "the children will be left all alone." The ambulance took my wife and Fadwa's body to the hospital.

Overcome with grief, Tayseer has to stop again. All of his children are gathered around him as he is speaks. He holds them tight and assures them that he loves them and that everything will be okay. A few minutes later, he continues.

I managed to make it to the hospital the next day. At around nine in the morning, they had her in surgery. She was there for hours. I had to go back to be with my children.

The Israeli hand grenade blew up the telephone lines as well. It was like me and my children were in a desert. We had no food, no water, no electricity, and we had no idea of the fate of their mother.

On the second and third day, the battles near our house intensified. Our house was shelled while we were inside and part of it collapsed. I had no idea how to raise kids alone, especially in such times. My children were holding onto me screaming and crying and saying they were scared. I did all I could to comfort them.

On the fourth day, I managed to sneak to my neighbor's house and speak to my wife on my neighbor's cell phone. I spoke with her and all of her children spoke to her. A heavy weight was lifted from my shoulders. She told me that they gave her a blood transfusion, six units. They also performed several surgeries, despite their lack of means.

She stayed in the Jenin hospital for twenty-seven days and was then transferred to Al-Makassed hospital in Jerusalem, where she stayed for another twenty days. Despite her frail condition, Israeli soldiers ordered her to exit the ambulance between Jenin and Jerusalem to be searched and so they could search the ambulance.

Fadwa died after being shot eight times. She was wearing a white nursing uniform, and she wore a badge for the Red Crescent Society. It was clear that she was a woman and a nurse. It was clear that she was no threat to them. She was shot with four bullets in the abdomen and four bullets in the chest. For me it was a double tragedy. It was the worst thing I have ever faced in my life. I feel like it was a test from God. I still don't understand how Fadwa could come to my house as a guest and leave a martyr.

Despite the destruction in the family's house, the home from inside is very clean and organized. The children are very polite. They sit quietly until you ask them a question about the incident, and then they politely answer with tears. They are always gathered around their mother and father. Three months after the incident, their mother is home again, and walks using crutches. Her children always offer to help her. Although a very sad atmosphere still engulfs the Damaj household, the family is stronger than ever.

Rafidia al-Jamal

Rafidia al-Jamal is a thirty-five-year-old mother of five. Her brother was killed during the first Intifada (1987-1991). She called her 13 year old daughter Jirah, which means "wounds", because of the sorrow she felt after her brother was killed. She is well educated and very articulate.

When the army first entered they took over the roofs of high buildings, and positioned themselves on the top of mosques. My sister is a nurse. She was assigned to work in one of the field hospitals that were set up in every area being invaded.

Around four in the morning, we heard the explosion of a shell. My sister was supposed to go to the hospital right away to help care for the wounded. This is why she left the house—especially after we heard people screaming for help. My sister was wearing her white uniform, and I was still in my nightgown. I put a scarf on my head and went to escort her as she crossed the street. Before we left, I asked her to wash for prayer. She had so much faith, especially in times like these. When the shell fell we did not feel any fear, we just knew that some people were in need of rescue.

When we went outside, some neighbors were also out. We asked them who was wounded. As we were talking with them, Israeli bullets began to fall on us like rain. I was wounded in my left shoulder. Israeli soldiers were positioned on the top of the mosque, and that was the direction from which the bullets came. I told my sister Fadwa that I was wounded. We were standing under a light post, so it was very clear who we were from the way we were dressed. But as she tried to help me, her head fell on me. She was showered with bullets. Fadwa fell on my leg and now I was lying on the ground. The bullet broke my leg. With her head resting on me I told her, "Make your prayers," because I knew she was going to die. I didn't expect her to die so fast though—she couldn't finish her prayers. Since then, I have been thinking of nothing but her. People will be talking to me and I'll be thinking about my sister. Everything in life, no matter how significant it might appear, compared to that moment is nothing. Before she died, I said to her, "Where is your wound, put your hand on your wound!" She couldn't. She tried to talk, and all that came out of her mouth was groaning.

Rafidia al-Jamal

Some people on the other side of the street wanted to come and help us.

"Stay there!" I told them.

"What happened?" they asked.

"My sister and I are wounded," I said, "and she cannot speak."

"Let us come and pull you to safety," they pleaded. I didn't want anyone else to die. I knew that my sister and I were going to die, and I wanted to die together. The Israelis were watching us from afar, but they continued to shoot at us. Another bullet entered my right leg, and one into my waist. I put my head on the ground and covered my head with my arms. I wasn't afraid. I felt that God was with me. I was sitting in a pool of blood. I didn't know who to worry about—myself, my sister, or those who wanted to come and help us. My husband was in the house with my children. When he tried to come out, they fired a shell at him. He shouted at me to come toward him. Instead I started going back. I just wanted to make sure he wouldn't approach and get killed. Finally I decided to crawl. I started crawling very slowly, but then they shot at me again. A bullet hit me in the chest. It took me ages to reach the gate of our house. All I could think of was Fadwa. Once I reached there, just the second my husband stepped outside to help me, another shell fell right beside him—but he got me in. He said he was going to get my sister. "Don't go," I told him, "she is dead."

My children came with towels to cover my wounds. My children were crushed. They were so afraid as they looked at me with blood covering my body. For two months, I was separated from my children. While I was in the hospital, they stayed for a few days with their father, then they spent the rest of the time with my family. We were all away from each other. My children have nightmares.

On that night when my sister was killed and I was wounded, the ambulance managed to reach us some hours later. They risked their lives to help us. They put my sister in the ambulance and my husband shouted at them, "My wife is wounded!" He carried me to the ambulance and ran back to be with my children. Just the moment the ambulance began moving, a shell fell near it. I was bleeding from six places on my body, and my sister was lying beside me dead. On the way to the hospital I drifted in and out of consciousness several times. Each time I would open my eyes, I would be looking at the face of my dead sister. My sister was twenty-seven years old. You can ask the nurses in the hospital about her, she was so kind. Some people say that God chose her to be a martyr because she was so kind. She was my best friend. At times I felt like a mother to her. I was always so excited when she would call and say that she was coming to visit. It has been three months since she died. There is so much sorrow in my heart, I just cannot convey my pain to anyone. I think about her every moment of my life.

Rafidia was permanently disabled from her wounds and needs the assistance of crutches to walk.

Ihab Ayadi

Ihab Ibrahim Ayadi (35) works for the Palestinian Red Crescent Society. He works in the relief and rescue department as a paramedic and in ambulance dispatch.

During the invasion in April, all the rescue teams in the area gathered. From the first until the fourth day of the invasion, we were notified of many casualties. We managed to enter the camp to help in the rescue and recovery efforts. Despite the Israeli army blockades and harassment, it was possible to enter the camp. Although Israeli tanks and airplanes kept targeting us, God was watching over us.

In only the first two days we recovered thirteen martyrs and fifty wounded. The wounded were suffering from very serious injuries, especially to the head, chest, and neck. The martyrs we recovered were civilians and resistance fighters.

At one point, I was taken out of my ambulance by Israeli soldiers. They humiliated and insulted me. Most of the harassment we endured during these days came from the "special forces" that took over people's homes. In the following days, we began facing serious problems reaching the wounded, especially in areas that were besieged and where heavy shelling was taking place. The panic people felt was also a problem. Some people would call, but they were so terrified and in shock that they could not explain what they needed. I used to park the ambulance near where we knew there were wounded, and then I would start running from home to home on foot to find the wounded. It took a long time to reach people's homes because of the firing and the blockade. We would finally arrive to find the wounded had bled to death.

Nidal Abu al-Hayjah was one of the people who bled very badly, and we could not reach him even though he was only a few feet from us. Nidal was wounded and was left to bleed behind his house. Around him were snipers. Anyone who attempted to help him was shot.

I received a call that there was a wounded person hit in the head by helicopter fire. They said he was bleeding very badly. Once I got close to the scene, I found him covered in blood from a terrible wound on his head. He was dead. I put him in the ambulance and we headed to the Jenin hospital. Along the way I looked in the rear view mirror, and I saw the Jenin hospital's ambulance behind me. He got closer and shouted to me that there was a bleeding man near the elementary school. I turned around and headed to the scene. I later learned that the ambulance driver who informed me of the wounded man came under fire, and had survived an Israeli attack thanks to a miracle. Anyway, I got close to the elementary school and found myself in an area that had been heavily attacked. I started walking through very small and narrow alleyways. One of the residents whispered to me from a window to watch for special forces that were hiding in that area and shooting at anything that moved. I looked to the sky, wary of any airplane that might have an easy shot at me. I couldn't find any. I managed to reach the wounded man. I proceeded carefully. On my hands and knees I touched his neck to look for a pulse and realized that, although he had lost a great amount of blood, he was still alive. I grabbed his arms and started to drag him to safety. As I was doing this, a man came running toward me very fast. The moment he was behind me, I heard a bullet. Then he fell and groaned, "I am wounded." I took him with me to the ambulance. I tore off his shirt and realized that blood was pouring out of his chest. My team and I tried to do all we could until we reached the hospital. On the way, I figured out why that man was running towards me: he had realized that I wasn't able to help the wounded man on my own and ran out of his house to help me. The bullet hit his heart. Two hours later he died. I can never forget this—not in all my life. I was in a state of shock for a long time. These two people who died with me were the last that I was able to attempt to rescue during the invasion.

The Israelis began blocking our way and firing at us. For example, on the third day of the invasion we worked under fire from three to five in the afternoon. Around five in the afternoon, I arrived at the *Zahrah* to rescue wounded, but there were some tanks blocking the ambulances' way. I thought that we were in the middle of a clash between Israeli soldiers and resistance fighters and tried to proceed, however, the tanks opened fire directly on us. You know, since the killing of Dr. Khalil at the hands of the Israelis, we have been very careful not to be on our own—we only travel in groups. This way, if one of us is shot, the other can rescue the injured. I didn't know what to do, there was a wounded man lying ten meters away from us and the Israelis were opening fire on the ambulance. Bullets were flying all around us. It was a very difficult thing to do, but we fled to the Jenin hospital. As we pulled in front of the hospital's gate, we received news that the Israelis took over the house of Dr. Malik Masoud, a physician who works at the Jenin hospital. His house was located beside the hospital. The army stationed itself inside his house, and whenever the ambulance would pull up to carry the wounded into the hospital, the army would open fire. Once we realized this, we opened the hospital doors and stormed into the hospital with the engine left running, the lights on, and the siren blaring. Just seconds after we stepped into the hospital, we turned around and found about twenty Israeli soldiers hiding near the gate of the hospital. They shouted at us, "Stop!"

I was nervous. I looked at their commander and said, "Hi, how can I help you?"

"Were you inside the camp?"

"Yes."

"Have you brought anybody with you?"

"I couldn't because the tanks started firing at us."

"Why? Haven't you coordinated with the Israeli forces?" I explained to him that the Israeli army was refusing to coordinate with the Red Crescent and the Red Cross Society. He ordered his troops to search the ambulance thoroughly. "You have brought this on yourself," he muttered.

"I am a paramedic and an ambulance driver," I replied. "All I care about is to rescue whomever is in need of help: a Jew, a foreigner, or a Palestinian. I was taught this."

He took my ID and brought me to the corner and said, "I want you to listen to this carefully. You are not allowed to move in or out of the camp, or to send one single ambulance anywhere without the prior permission of the army. Whoever disobeys these orders will be shot. Any breaking of the rules and we will hold you responsible."

"But sometimes there are critical cases where we cannot wait for written consent," I said.

"These are the orders," he said. "Obey them or bear the consequences."

For two days, the soldiers held us in the hospital. People would call us, reporting wounded all across the camp, but we could not move. If we dared to leave, soldiers would immediately open fire, and we had to go back to the hospital for cover. Then they started shelling the hospital. They bombed the oxygen room. They bombed the day care. We began running out of food and medicine. This was very difficult on us and on

Ihab Ibrahim A'yadi and his clearly marked vehicle

the people of Jenin. On one occasion, we were told that a house caught on fire after it was attacked by an Apache helicopter. A whole family burned inside, but we couldn't get to them.

I love my job. It is so rewarding when you feel that you can save lives. But answering telephone calls from people screaming that their loved ones are bleeding to death, while you cannot go to help, left me in a state of shock. I was one of many who wept those days because of the helplessness I felt.

On one occasion I wanted to test the soldiers. I took one of the crew and moved toward the ambulance. We heard a few shots in the air but we didn't run, we stood there. Suddenly the commander of the unit that raided the hospital two days earlier came to me. He came with a smirk on his face and said, "What's going on, Ihab?"

"What are you so happy about?" I asked. "We have people dying and we cannot reach them." I implored him and finally, we reached an agreement allowing us to move within a limited area specified by the soldiers. At that point, we were not aware of anything happening in the camp. We did know that there were many wounded and many deaths, but we didn't know where exactly. Those who had been calling and begging us to come and help had stopped calling.

In any case, we decided to enter the camp. According to the agreement, we went to the checkpoint. The soldiers searched our ambulance for two hours. But just as we entered the camp, bullets flew all around the ambulance. We fled. The army claimed that the Palestinian fighters were firing at us. Nonsense. The Palestinians had wounded who they wanted to evacuate. The army prevented me from using the siren. When we used to do that before, the people of Jenin would come out with their wounded. But now they didn't know we were in the area, and it was too dangerous for anyone to step outside to look for us, so we came back to the hospital. I went back to the soldiers stationed near the hospital.

"We have thirteen dead bodies in the hospital," I told them. "The refrigerator only has the capacity for three bodies. The bodies are decomposing and the smell is horrid." Eventually the number of martyrs went up to fifteen. Still, they wouldn't allow us to bury them. So we asked permission to bury them in the back of the hospital in the garden. We were told that as long as we stayed within the boundaries of the hospital property, we could bury them. But as we stepped out carrying the bodies, soldiers started firing at us. We ran back inside and decided that all of us should exit together, doctors, nurses, maintenance staff and pharmacists. We all wore white. We put the martyrs in plastic bags and found a few bricks to mark the graves. We wrote a name and number on each bag and we buried them—just temporarily we thought. The director of the hospital was the one who drove the machine to dig the graves. We rested a little, and I went back to the soldiers and begged, "For God's sake, allow us entry into the camp."

"You can send three cars," the commander finally said, "but you have to coordinate every move with us." We loaded three ambulances with a crew and volunteers. But as we reached the Zahrah School, a tank blocked our way. There were a number of tanks and many soldiers. One of the soldiers stepped toward the ambulance I was in.

"Come over here," he said.

I stepped out of the car and he ordered me to take my clothes off. I told him in Hebrew, "I am going to rescue the wounded."

"Forbidden!" he replied.

I looked around me and I realized that there were over a thousand people just down the street: men, women, and children. The men were all stripped naked, blindfolded, and handcuffed. They were being dragged one by one to a place out of sight behind the brick factory. The children and the women looked hungry and exhausted from the heat. Most of them were barefoot. Seeing them reminded me of the Palestinians who were driven from their homes in 1948. Once the people realized I was an ambulance driver, it was like I was their gift from heaven. Many started weeping all at once, saying, "Please come over here!" They said, "There are people bleeding here!" I told the soldier, "Listen, this is beyond inhumane! I am a respected medical worker, don't humiliate me like this. You can either tie me and drag me into the brick factory with the others or let me go." He finally said, "Okay, put your clothes on and leave."

I realized what they were doing. They were trying to get all of the women and children out of the camp, so that they could topple the entire camp on the heads of the men. They wanted to kill them all. On my way back to the ambulance I shouted at the soldiers, "You cannot let thousands of innocent people walk out like this! The town of Jenin itself is under military curfew and the soldiers will definitely open fire on them!" They wouldn't listen. They didn't care. Immediately, I phoned the hospital administration. I told them that we had to find a way to shelter these people. I told them that we would have space for hundreds of people at the Red Crescent Center. Then I rushed back to the hospital. I took most of the volunteers, and we went to the Red Crescent to get things ready. When the volunteers saw the scene of people leaving the camp, they all started weeping.

We had some milk and water at the Red Crescent Center. I got things as ready as possible and sneaked back to the camp where I located three wounded. They had their hands and legs blown off. Some of them had been bleeding for three days. It was very painful. The soldiers caught us as we left the camp and held us for an hour and a half. Finally, they allowed us to take one of the wounded to the hospital. They left the two others in the blazing sun. Once we got to the hospital, I rushed the wounded man in. He was also bleeding from his head. Fifteen minutes after we got there, soldiers came running in, shouting at me. I was no longer afraid. "Let them do whatever they want to me," I thought. There were ten soldiers shouting at me all at once, and I shouted back. They were trying to seize the wounded from the hospital. I thought I would rather let the wounded die with me in dignity than to die in a military jeep, humiliated and abused. The soldiers have no regard for God's law.

Finally, the soldiers were distracted with something, and I managed to hide the wounded in a room where they could not find them. Two hours later, the other two wounded, who were left in the sun, were brought to the hospital in another ambulance. Just as they pulled into the hospital's emergency parking lot, soldiers came running. They arrested the wounded. They pulled the medical workers out of the ambulance. They beat them and threw them on the ground. By the time I came running out they had my colleague Ghassan in handcuffs. I also saw other people from the neighborhood handcuffed and sitting in the army jeeps. They even ordered one of the volunteers to strip other people. It was as if I completely lost my mind. Their commander, who refers to himself as Captain Jamal, is one of those responsible for the Jenin area. I looked at him and said, "What do you think you are doing?"

"Didn't we have an agreement to search all ambulances before they enter the hospital?" he said.

"You are supposed to be an educated man," I said. "What kind of logic is this? How can I leave people to bleed to death in the ambulance while your soldiers interrogate them and strip them naked? If you have a bit of humanity, you will release these poor people you have arrested."

"How can I tell who is wanted and who is not?" he said.

"For goodness sake," I said, "these are old women and children!" I also told him that we were already understaffed, "How can you use our volunteers to strip people?" Eventually, he gave me my ID and gave my colleagues their IDs back.

"Take your ambulances and staff," he said, "and leave this area—and don't let me see you again."

Some days later it became easier for us to work because the Red Crescent and the United Nations managed to coordinate with the Israelis. Our ambulances, however, still could not reach the hospital. We had to take the wounded to another clinic, and from there the wounded would be put on a cart and pushed all the way to hospital on foot. Women giving birth would have to give birth in the street. The soldiers stood and looked at us from afar.

Later I was stationed at the Red Crescent Center. Since we were not allowed to move about, we slept in the Center. We would sleep in our clothes after a very hard day of work. We had no water, and the situation was growing dire. There were over 200 families trapped with us. One day the soldiers came and surrounded the area. They asked about the driver of the ambulance, which was me. I came out. They searched the ambulance very thoroughly. They took my ID and said, "You are not allowed to carry any wounded in this ambulance."

The families inside the Center wanted to leave badly. There was no food or water for anyone. Around eight in the evening, when the Israelis finally allowed them to leave, people started running out of the Center with no sense of direction. They poured into the main street, but the Israeli forces wouldn't allow them to move. The commander came and he said, "They need to walk in a line, two by two."

Finally, the Red Crescent was able to bring some bottles of water. We gave the people some water and milk, and we instructed them how and where they should move. Al-Qade mosque in the town of Jenin opened its doors to host as many families as possible. Just as we managed to temporarily resolve the problem of those hundreds of homeless, the process started all over again as more than 800 people came pouring out of the camp. This time the shelters included charities, schools, and the municipality.

I was so consumed in this process that I did not realize what was happening in the background. The Israeli soldiers were arresting all of my colleagues. A soldier ordered me to approach. He shouted, "You are under arrest, take your clothes off!" All of my colleagues were also handcuffed. They took us to a detention center, where we were tortured for a whole day. We were left in the sun and dust, handcuffed and exhausted. In the middle of the night, they tied us together in large line, like a chain gang. They took us to Salem to be interrogated. In the interrogation, I kept telling them that they could not treat us this way, for we were medical workers. Finally, they released us, but they said we were forbidden to go back to Jenin. They said we could go to the villages on the outskirts. We went there for four days until the Red Cross came and escorted us back. This is our story.

The Head of the Palestinian Red Crescent Society Emergency Medical Service (EMS) in Jenin, Dr. Khalil Sulieman, 58, was killed by tank on March 4, 2002 while he was evacuating an injured girl in his ambulance from the Jenin refugee camp. He was alive for an hour and a half after having been shot. Israeli forces prevented him from receiving medical attention.

Muhanad Wishahe

Muhanad Essa Wishahe (12) is a student who was born and raised in the Jenin refugee camp. Family members stated that he was severely scarred by his experience during the Jenin invasion. He often does not sleep and his progress at school is hampered. He is constantly fearful, especially of seeing blood. He doesn't eat much and he is depressed. He has been isolating himself since the invasion took place. Throughout the interview, this young boy exhibited many signs of severe anxiety and deep sadness.

My mother was baking bread for the *shebab*. And she was baking them some sweets. Then heavy firing started in the Hawashin neighborhood where most of my family and I live. There was heavy firing beside our home. My mother looked out of the window, and when she did that, the Israelis opened fire at her. She was martyred when shrapnel hit her in the head and right here.

Muhanad touches his chest.

When she was first hit, me and my father tried to call the ambulance. My father ran outside the house to stop the ambulance when it came, so the Israelis started firing at him. Israeli soldiers close to us tried to scare him too, "Get inside your house!" they shouted.

My father continued to beg the soldiers to allow the ambulance to come and rescue my mother. "Sure the ambulance is coming," the soldiers would sometimes say. But sometimes they would laugh and start making fun of us, saying, "No Hamas, no Fatah, it's all gone!"

It wasn't long before we were running out of food, and could only eat one meal a day. Later, the Israeli soldiers gathered the people of the neighborhood here.

Muhanad points to the center courtyard of his home.

We asked them for an ambulance and the Israeli soldiers said, "No ambulances." One of the soldiers ordered us to get out of the house, but when we tried to carry my mother with us they ordered, "Leave her there, leave her there!"

Then we were told that children under the age of fifteen should go to the Red Crescent Center. I went, but my mother stayed home.

I learned that most of the army left our neighborhood hours later and only five soldiers remained. Then these soldiers left too, but they still did not allow the ambulance to come. My mother suffered for two days in our home, and then she finally bled to death.

The soldiers ordered everyone else to leave the camp. People started coming out of their homes holding white flags. But my uncle was very ill and could not walk. We tried to find something to carry him on, but we could not find anything, until some people brought a broken wooden door. We carried him on this.

When I was leaving the camp, I met a young man, Juma Abu Khalifah*, and he was wounded. Israeli soldiers were stomping on his legs and harassing him, saying, "You are Hamas, aren't you!"

Just as we started walking down the road, the Israelis started shouting at us, "Go back, go back!" So we all sat in a large group near one of the camp's homes. The Israelis would not let us move, and they would not allow us to bring my uncle to the hospital.

A neighbor lady of ours told me that my brother Muneer was martyred. My father did not know then. That's when I started looking for my brother Muneer. I found my brothers Thaer, Louay, and Abdullah. I also found my father looking for my brother among the young men gathered there. But neither one of us were able to find him. When my father came to the Red Crescent Center, he was told that my brother Muneer was martyred.

Muhanad's mother and eighteen-year-old brother Muneer remained in the camp, and their bodies were buried without the family present. The burial took place long after the bodies had decomposed.

*More than one eyewitness indicated that Abu Khalifah was wounded during the Israeli attack on the camp. He was left to bleed for several days without allowing an ambulance to reach him. When the Israeli army managed to penetrate the camp, they entered and found the young man in someone's home. They refused to treat him and threw him in the camps center square. He was arrested and taken to an unknown destination.

Fyrial al-Shalabi

A mother of 6, Fyrial Abdel Latif Yusuf al-Shalabi (28) is a beautifully fair, strong-willed woman. Her outspokenness does not hide the look of anguish in her eyes. Her love for her children seems to govern her words. She says that they give her a reason for living. She lives with her children in a very small and humble house. Following the Israeli invasion the house is severely damaged and is at risk of collapse. Despite these terrible living conditions, she still insists on sending her children to school. She lives in the Jurit Al-Dahab neighborhood, located in the center of Jenin's refugee camp. Fyrial currently has no form of income.

When the Israeli attack on the camp first started, I remained in the house with my husband and children. Tank shells started falling all around our house, and warplanes opened fire. We were terrified. We took our children and fled to my in-laws' house, located in the Sahah, just beside the United Nations health clinic. We stayed there from Wednesday until Saturday. On Saturday, the army came to my in-laws' house and ordered all of us to go out into the street. So we did. They searched us, and then they brought us to a neighbors house with two other families. We were twenty-two people, in one small room. But before they locked the door, they took my husband, Waddah, our neighbor Abdelkarim al-Sadi and my father in-law. They ordered them to stand outside beside the main door of the house.

Fyrial pauses for a moment. Her eyes flood with tears, she holds her young child close to her breast, and proceeds.

You know, they never did anything wrong. But they were searched again, and they compared their names to a long list of men wanted by the Israeli army. All three men were carrying young children with them. The soldiers snatched the children and sent them back inside the house. After a few moments we heard heavy firing, we did not know who was being fired at since the army locked us up in that small room. It was shortly after sunset. We had no idea if they had been killed until eleven-thirty that night, when we decided to break out of the room. We found them all dead. The soldiers were not there. We called the ambulance, but the army would not let medical relief into the camp. My husband's body laid in the street for four days. We were not allowed to bring him inside to safety. Every time we tried to pull the bodies of the men inside, the soldiers would open fire. After those four days, using loudspeakers the Israelis ordered the people to leave and go to Al-Iskan. (Al-Iksan is a newer housing development in the town of Jenin where many families fled until the end of the attack.)

My husband's body was left outside for another six days. We had him wrapped in a blanket and laid a piece of cardboard over him to protect him. It was a total of twelve days before he was buried. My husband was a student at the university. He would have graduated in one month. He was supporting our family by working as a security guard in the Haifa school.

Fighting more tears, Fyrial sighs heavily and then continues.

He was the only supporter of our family. I have six children that I must care for. The oldest is ten years old and the youngest is six months old. What am I supposed to do?

Fathi al-Shalabi

Fathi Saleh Abdullah al-Shalabi is a sixty-three-year-old clerk in the Jenin Municipality. He works for the utilities department. Following his experiences during the Israeli invasion, he said that his life is completely changed. He hardly smiles and is easily angered. He has a yellowish, thin face, he struggles to focus and finds it difficult to recall the events. It took us a week to interview him, because he kept avoiding us. He has spoken to journalists a lot, but he has reached the conclusion that nobody seems to care. He lives in a house located near the center of the camp. He has difficulty hearing and uses a hearing aid in his left ear. He has a family of eight.

On the sixth of April, around six-thirty in the evening the Israeli army began searching house to house in the area where I live. My son Waddah came to my house with his wife and his six children. Their oldest is ten and their youngest is six months. He lives nearby, just 150 meters up the street. He works for the Hittin school. He also was a student in the Open University in Jerusalem and he was prepared to receive his BA in April.

The Israeli soldiers were approaching a house very close to ours. Abdelkarim al-Sadi our neighbor was knocking on our door. I didn't know what he wanted exactly, but we asked him if he knew where the army was. "They are searching our house," he said. We insisted that he stay with us because we felt that his life would be in danger if he went back. My son Waddah, Abdelkarim, I, and nearly twenty more people were in one room. The army finished searching his house and then moved to Abu Amer's house. Once they began searching Abu Amer's house, I think they heard the voices of the children. They came and they ordered us all out. "Stand over here," they commanded. We stood for five minutes while they pointed their machine guns at us. They ordered us to walk in front of them. My son was carrying a baby in his arms. Abdelkarim was carrying a little girl, she was only two and a half. They singled me, Waddah and Abdelkarim out. They took the children away from us and ordered them back into the house. They took all of the women and the children and put them in one room in Abu Abed's house and locked them in. Me, Waddah and Abdelkarim stayed out, they would not let us in with our families. Three soldiers remained with us. The rest of them were searching other peoples' homes. The soldiers ordered us to lift our shirts up. Once we did, one of the soldiers shouted in Hebrew, "Kill them!" and they started shooting at us. I fell on the ground. I put my hands on my face. Other soldiers thought that they were being shot at, so they threw themselves on the ground and started shooting. The women and the children inside had no idea what was happening. The soldiers thought that I was dead. The blood of my son and my neighbor was gushing down toward me. I pretended that I was dead. Their blood covered me. The soldiers thought that the blood was mine. They didn't check to see if we were dead or alive, they just assumed that we were all killed. We stayed for hours that way. One of the guards once in a while would approach us and would shine his flashlight on us. But I continued to pretend that I was dead. One of them stood on my right shoulder, that hurt me very much, but I wouldn't move.

Once the guards walked away, I tried to see if my son was still alive. I finally was able to reach his hand. It was then I knew that he had been martyred. I managed to crawl on my hands and knees toward Abu Amer's house. It was dark, and the air raids were still continuing. Abu Amer was surprised to see me because he too heard the soldier shouting in Hebrew, "Kill them!" And he saw the shooting. I changed my clothes and kept going from one room to the other. I was worried that once the soldiers realized that one of the dead people was missing, they would turn the area upside down to find me and kill me. I saw two of my neighbors trying to cover my son and Abdelkarim with blankets. I also heard them asking, "Where is the third martyr?" "Maybe he managed to crawl inside one of the houses to die," suggested a neighbor. I opened the door and whispered to them that I was still alive. The soldiers were convinced that I was also dead. For three days my son and Abdelkarim were lying outside, where the tanks would pass by them very fast. I was looking at them from the window, unable to pull them in.

On the fourth day, the Israeli army called on loudspeakers to the people to evacuate their homes. I managed to return home. The women insisted on looking at the faces of the two martyrs. Once we saw the way their bodies looked after four days the women wept and they pulled their hair.

The soldiers gathered us in a building that was used by the Palestinian police, and is now destroyed. I was in a group of nearly sixty people. It was a mixed group including children and elderly. I managed to sneak to an area near the northern entrance of the camp where my sister lives. My sister's name is Kharoubi. I stayed there for ten days. When I came back after the massacre, I could not find my son's body. The neighbors told me that an ambulance took my son and Abdelkarim just two days before.

I went to the hospital and I asked them about my son. They said, "We don't have names, but we buried many people in the hospital's backyard, just temporarily." A few days later,

Fathi Saleh Abdullah al-Shalabi

I returned to the hospital and I found them taking the bodies out of the mass grave. They were putting them in bags, and writing their names on the bags. They put them in trucks and put them in another mass grave in the camp's graveyard. I am still not certain where my son was buried, because he was buried with many others. This is all I can tell you. All that we can do is to ask God to be merciful and to give us patience and faith. Our life is very hard.

As hospital personnel were transporting the bodies from the hospital yard to the graveyard, the al-Shalabi family was prevented from seeing the body of their son Waddah because of the condition of the body—it had been laying in the street for ten days. Overwhelmed with sorrow, Waddah's mother fainted when she realized that she could not say her final good byes to her son.

71

Sana al-Sadi

Sana al-Sadi (18) is a short, fair teenager who wears a simple dress and a head scarf. She was very shy when we first began, but then her brave spirit emerged. Her eyes are full of sadness. Her house is located in the center of the camp. She constantly wears black.

I married my husband Abdelkarim Yusuf al-Sadi just recently. I had never met him before. It was an arranged marriage. Abdelkarim and I had a very happy life together, although it was cut too short.

During the invasion, I was at my in-laws' house with my husband. We were all sitting together as the area was being shelled by the Israelis. We constantly tried to comfort each other. Some women in the neighborhood said I should leave the camp. I said, "We are going nowhere, this is our camp and we should stay." My husband used to tease me, saying, "I am afraid that with your attitude, you will end up in jail." I used to ask him, "Wouldn't you love to be a resistance fighter?" He would say, "I am happy the way I am." He didn't like to listen to the news and wasn't very engaged in what was going on.

During the first day, I spent the time trying to cheer everyone up. Our neighbors escaped to our house when the shells destroyed their home. They came and they were crying. I tried to cheer them up, but it was hopeless. Everyone was upset. They didn't eat and the children would wet themselves from fear and wet their beds at night. When an airplane would come and start bombing, the children would cling to their mothers and scream.

We were many people in the house. My father-in-law was there, a neighbor of ours, my mother-in-law, my cousins and of course many of our neighbors. Our neighbors stayed with us for two days.

The Israeli soldiers came and blasted open the back gate. They started shouting, "Open the door! Open the door!" My father-in-law ran out and unlocked the door. The Israelis stormed in. They ordered all the people in the house to assemble. They had us sit in the mint garden in the backyard. I was sitting with my two cousins. My mother-in-law was too sick to move, so she stayed where she was. For some reason, I started to laugh uncontrollably, I don't know why.

More Israeli soldiers gathered in the house. There were so many of them—over sixty, I would say. They made my father-in-law go upstairs with them to search the upper floors. Then the soldiers took me and my cousins and locked us inside a room. They also locked up our neighbor's family with us. It was dark in there, the soldiers would shout at us if we tried to talk. One of the women who was brought in told me that my husband and some other men were all standing outside. The number of people in the room grew to nearly twenty. We were sitting on top of each other because the room was so small.

At that point, people tell me that Abdelkarim my husband, Waddah al-Shalabi, our neighbor and his father were ordered to stand outside near a wall. They were ordered to lift up their arms while facing the wall. As they did so, the soldiers opened fire to execute all three of them. We just heard the gunfire. The Israeli soldiers inside the house thought that they were being fired upon, so they rushed inside the room and hid behind us and behind the children. They started yelling, "Outside! Outside!" But once they found out that it was the other soldiers that were firing, they were at ease.

We had no idea what was happening. It was nearly eleven at night. We did not know that they were killed. We knew that these three men had nothing to do with the resistance. We did not expect that they would be executed. We just thought that they would be taken as human shields. We sat quietly until the next day, only the children managed to sleep. We were still locked in. They also tied the doors with ropes.

I was dying from worry. I said, "I'm going outside to check." But I couldn't open the door. Our neighbor jumped out of the window, and opened the door for us. The soldiers were not there. The neighbor said, "Three martyrs are lying outside." My father-in-law went out and he saw that it was Abdelkarim, Waddah and his father. When he came back, he didn't tell us right away, instead he took some of the neighbors aside and started talking to them. I wondered why he didn't come to talk to me or to Waddah's family. I knew something terrible had happened and my father-in-law was seeking the help of our neighbors to tell us the bad news. But I rushed outside and saw Abdelkarim and Waddah lying dead. Waddah's father was not there. We did not know that he was still alive. I was so angry, I wished that I could have seen some soldiers then. I would have strangled them.

I went and I held Abdelkarim's hand. I cradled his head in my arms and looked at him. His head was opened and part of his neck was also open. My sister-in-law started screaming, "Father! Father! This is your son!" But Abdelkarim's father was in a state of shock. I started screaming at the top of my lungs, "They have died, they have been martyred!" My mother-in-law couldn't move, so she asked me, "What happened to them, tell me!" I said, "They were just wounded and taken by the ambulance." She said, "You are lying to me, you just said they have been martyred!" Some of the children fainted and fell. Waddah's son is less than one year old. He started crying and spoke his first word, "Baba, baba." His mother held him, "Couldn't you have said it to your father before he died?" she said.

My husband was so innocent. He never hurt anyone. I was so terrified and humiliated. I immediately felt like I wanted to avenge my husband.

Before the invasion we were talking about the name we should give to our child, with whom I was pregnant. He wanted to call him "Kassem," if it is a boy. I am still pregnant, I am not sure, but I think I have a baby girl in my belly. I would like to call her "Zuhur," which means "flowers." Maybe one day our life will change for the better. I want to raise Abdelkarim's daughter to have the best life and to receive the best education.

Nael Ammar

Nael Ammar is married with five children. The forty-three-year-old has been unemployed since the eruption of the Palestinian uprising two years ago. He lives in the Masjid neighborhood in the center of the camp, near the Sahah. He is short and sturdy. He has a strong personality and precise memory. Nael is well educated and has a very strong disposition and way of expressing himself. He is a former political prisoner and has been in several Israeli jails. His eyes sparkle with courage and determination. His expressions make his listeners feel that his hardship will do nothing but make him stronger. He spent many years building his own home, but it is now in disrepair due to Israeli shelling.

A week before the invasion, the people of Jenin were preparing. During the last invasion the Israeli army blew up the water supply, preventing the people from drinking. So we were storing up barrels of water. We collected some first aid supplies and also stocked up on medicines, especially if a family member had a chronic disease. Our aim was to live as long as possible under the siege. In past invasions the Israelis invaded for one or two days and then left. This time, however, we miscalculated. I also think that the Israelis miscalculated. Maybe they thought that once a great number of tanks and soldiers invaded the camp the *shebab* would run away or give themselves up. But the *shebab* decided to fight, and the residents of the camp also decided to stay put. Neither we or the Israeli army had guessed right. The invasion began toward dawn on a Tuesday. It was pouring down rain. The army began shelling using heavy machine guns mounted on tanks that were stationed on the outskirts of the camp. Apache helicopters hovered over the camp ahead of the tanks. Then the helicopters began to attack, using heavy machine guns and missiles.

Our house is located on a relatively wide street. The street is easy for a tank to pass through. From this street, it is easy for the Israelis to take charge during the first hours of any battle. Despite this, they couldn't manage to enter the camp until the fourth day because the resistance was too strong. Also, the *shebab* booby-trapped some of the large streets to prevent the tanks from advancing. On the fourth day, they managed to enter because the tank had a minesweeper on it. This giant tank could simply run over the booby traps, especially since they were very primitive booby-traps. The explosives were normally attached to a wire, and if you cut the wire, you would disable the explosives. That's why they brought very large bulldozers and simply crushed all of the booby traps. Most of them didn't even detonate. Once the army took over our street, they started shooting missiles from the air. We feared that the more the fighting continued, the more savage they would become in their treatment of the residents of the camp.

On the fifth day they started shelling homes. A large number of people were killed or wounded. My neighbor's home was blown up by missiles. When my neighbors' son started shouting for help, I tried to help him, but there was an Israeli sniper nearby—over there.

He points to the opposite side of the street.

When I opened the door, he began shooting at us. It was like a rain of bullets. An Apache came and fired toward my house. I knew that the neighbor boy was wounded. I called the ambulance, but the Red Crescent's ambulance was blocked at the entrance of the camp by the Israeli soldiers. They told us over the phone to put some salted water on the boy's wounds, and to tie it to a splint. At that point, the third floor of the neighbor's house was on fire and the Israelis were still shelling. A missile landed on the second floor of my house, but thank God, it did not explode. My house was full of shrapnel and parts of exploded and unexploded missiles.

We saw more foot soldiers come into the camp. They were entering in groups, perhaps twenty at a time. We were terrified and afraid that they would enter the homes and kill everybody because we knew that some people from the neighborhood were taken by the soldiers and killed in the street. We kept our faith, and we resisted until the eighth day.

On the eighth day the army called on loudspeakers and ordered us to leave our homes. The first thing I did was to go to the remains of my neighbor's home and help his wounded son. Many of us took the boy and left. We were forced to set the wounded boy at a checkpoint located between the town of Jenin and the refugee camp. The soldiers took us one by one and ordered us to take off all our clothes, everything except our underwear. There was a young boy, his name is Imad and he was wearing a long jacket. As we were walking, they screamed at him and ordered him to stop. Imad didn't understand what they wanted so they loaded their weapons and are about to start shooting. They were speaking in Hebrew and I understood what they wanted. I too started to scream at the boy, "Stop, they are going to kill you!" I told him, "Take off your jacket and sit on the ground!"

We were mostly older people, sick and wounded. We had nine handicapped people with us, three were from the same family, sons of Abu Ibrahim. Some of us were very old and some were senile. When the soldiers commanded them to go left, out of confusion they would go right. But the soldiers stripped them naked anyway. I tried to help them as much as I could. I was the only one who spoke Hebrew.

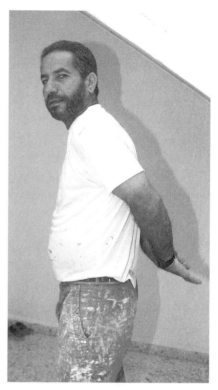

Nael Ammar

Close to us was a group of young men. They were handcuffed, naked, and lying on their stomachs. The Israeli tanks would roar past them at high speed, only forty centimeters away from their heads. Imagine the horror that they must have felt. Then they began tying us up, one by one. They ordered us to lie on our stomachs. Of course, they didn't even do that the easy way. They would take each one of us and force us onto the ground, stomping on our backs and heads. One soldier would put his machine gun right on your head and the other would tie you up.

We were in very painful positions. We begged them for a chance to move a little. I told one of the soldiers, "Let me speak with your commander." He said, "What do you want?" I told him, "When you asked us to leave our homes, we expected that you would treat us with some respect, but you are treating us like dogs. Even your dog is running around free. We are old, handicapped and sick, yet are forced to lie naked on the ground. I would rather go home and have your Apache blow up my house while I am inside, than be treated like a dog." He looked at me and said, *"Sheket,"* which means "shut up." He said we would have to wait for two more hours. We had some wounded with us, they were shivering and in pain.

Hours later, we began our trip to Salem, the headquarters for the Israeli intelligence and military administration. This is often where Palestinians are taken to be interrogated. They carried us in military buses, and told us that we could not sit down. The buses stopped near the main entrance of Jenin, near Haifa Street. There they switched the way our hands were tied. We had them tied in the back, and they tied them in the front. They blindfolded us, and transported us in Israeli army jeeps. We were met by two soldiers who treated us savagely. They beat us ruthlessly when we were blindfolded. They beat me endlessly here.

He points to the top of his head.

They hit me so hard there that I could hardly hear anything. Even now, my right ear still hurts. I kept telling them, "I'm a civilian." One of the soldiers said, "We ordered you to leave four days ago and you didn't." I said, "You were calling on the fighters and we aren't fighters. Neither me nor my wife, nor my children have anything to do with the battle."

It was a long time before we arrived in Salem. We had a mute young man with us. The young man was screaming awful screams—muffled, but dreadful screams. It seems that his hands were bleeding because his handcuffs were so tight. The soldiers were annoyed. They barked, "What's wrong with him?" I said, "He is mute and he is in pain." They responded, "We should be there soon."

Eventually we arrived at an area where we were interrogated one by one. After that, all of us were put in a caged area. There was no tent and it was very cold. They threw only one blanket and one small bottle of water at us, yet we were nearly 170 people. They brought us an old barrel to use as a toilet. The barrel was so high that it was impossible to use it for anything but urinating. Some of the people with us were already sick, they had terrible stomach pain. It was most difficult on the wounded since they already had so much to worry about.

We had six wounded, one of them had his finger cut off by shrapnel. Many times we implored the soldiers to allow a doctor to see him, but they would say, "Later, later." Then his finger turned green, and the flies wouldn't leave him alone. Then his entire hand started to swell. "He is going to die from gangrene!" I shouted at the soldiers.

A soldier approached us, "You are all terrorists! You all make bombs

80

and throw them at the army!" he shouted at us in Hebrew.

I told him that this was not true. "We are ordinary people, we were staying in our homes," I said, "and you came, and you dragged us out at gunpoint." The soldier got angry, he pulled a gun and wanted to shoot me. But one of his commanders ordered him to stop.

We stayed there. Every so often, a soldier would emerge from a tent to unleash his anger on us. Another soldier just wanted to shoot us. He pleaded with his commander in Hebrew, "Let me kill just two, it's not a big deal." He spoke as if our lives had no value. This just shows you how hateful they are, and how they see us, lives that have less value than animals.

During the night it became very cold. They brought each of us one small blanket. It still wasn't enough for any warmth. Should we use them for pillows, or should we cover our bodies with them? In any case, we gave our blankets to the wounded, so they would have at least two. We stayed that way until one in the morning. Then we were taken again, one by one, to be interrogated. They decided to send us to another jail called Ofra. In Ofra, they also left us with no food, and did not allow us to go to the bathroom. Finally, they brought us something to eat, a small container of yogurt, half a cucumber and one tomato. This was to be shared among four men.

On the fifth day, they allowed us to have some water and soap. From Ofra, they took us to the Megiddo prison.

We stayed for 20 days in Megiddo. It was better for us there because there were other Palestinian prisoners who took care of us. They shared some of their clothes with us. That is all I have to say.

Nawal Hawashin

Nawal Mazin Hawashin (38) is very thin and frail looking, yet she is strong-minded. She wears a very simple traditional Palestinian dress. It is apparent that she lives under very difficult financial and psychological circumstances. She has eight children, and her husband, Mazin, works for the health department in the Jenin municipality. Their house consists of two rooms and a kitchen, located in the Jurit Al-Dahab neighborhood. She speaks hurriedly and frequently makes gestures with her hands when she talks, especially when she is sad. She often gets angry.

We heard that the Israeli army began to invade the camp on the news. My husband was sick and was outside the camp, but I remained at home with my children. We were very scared. The neighbors called us and said, "Come and sleep with us tonight." We stayed at the home of Abu Iyad Nasser for three days, and in the home of Abu Hisham for one night, until Abu Hisham's home was shelled. We didn't want to burden them, so we left for the home of Abu Ziad and stayed there three nights. My children were so scared. They were crying all the time, crying but trying to be quiet, so the soldiers would not hear them. The boys were terrified, but they were ashamed of saying so. One of the children lost the hearing in one of his ears from the loud sound of the bombing. I put a few drops of olive oil in his ear to help him.

Nawal grabs her son Ali, kisses him, and holds him tight to her breast before she continues.

One night we were sleeping. At around two in the morning, we woke up to the sound of airplane shelling. Immediately we washed and started to pray for God's protection.

Early that morning, we saw Israeli soldiers coming into our neighborhood, and the nearby Sumran neighborhood. They had bulldozers and began demolishing the homes. They destroyed one neighbor's home and then they went to the home of Ziad al-Sayadaly. The soldiers told Ziad, "If we find anything inside your house we are going to blow it up with you inside."

By that time, we had returned home from our neighbors. Soldiers came and pounded on the door of our home. I heard them asking someone, "Whose house is this?" That person answered, "It's Mazin al-Hawashin's, and his wife and children are inside." I came running and opened the door. They were slamming the gate door so hard that I couldn't open it. After a struggle, I managed to open it. One of the soldiers hit me on the back with the butt of his rifle and ordered me to walk in front of him. There were more than a dozen of them, and they made me walk in front of them, opening the doors. They entered my home and pushed me into the living room. They began wrecking and destroying everything. Then they ordered me to move to other rooms. In every room we would enter, they would begin to destroy it and turn it upside down. They left nothing intact. Then they left the house. I asked if I could close the gate. "No," they said, "you are going to come and open your neighbor's door for us."

"I am only responsible for my home," I explained. But then they started to hit me on the back.

I went knocking on other doors. The first door I knocked at was Jamal al-Rakh's. There was no one inside. They asked where he was and I said that maybe he was in the hospital. I said, "Why won't you just leave me alone?" But they forced me to keep on walking. I saw them destroying the house of Abu Hassan Mahdi. The soldiers with me were walking very close, I think they were afraid that the *shebab* would throw something at them. When I saw them destroying the house of Abu Hassan, I told them to fear God. One of the soldiers said in broken Arabic, "We are destroying his house because he did not open his door." They forced me to walk in front of all twelve of them. We turned around a corner and I was shocked to see three soldiers lying on their stomachs, aiming to shoot. Their machine guns were pointed at Abu Ziad's house. I told them I would not pass in front of them because I was afraid they might shoot me. When the soldiers who were lying on their stomachs allowed me to pass, I got so scared I started to run. They all started laughing at me. I knocked at the doors of more homes, and an hour later they allowed me to return home.

We stayed that night at Abu Ziad's house. We woke up at dawn to loudspeakers ordering us to leave our homes because they were going to raze the camp. Many of the people of Jurit Al-Dahab started fleeing their homes. We realized that the people of the Damaj neighborhood were also moving toward us holding white flags. We moved in large groups. I

84

took some bread and a bag with the birth certificates of my children and passports—all the important papers related to my children. Just a few blocks after we began walking, I saw the soldiers digging a large hole in the ground, taking mud from one area and moving it to another. The soldiers said, "All the women with bags, throw them into the street!" I was very afraid for the safety of my children, especially since I had my seventeen-year-old son Muhammad with me. They ordered my son and other young men to take off all their clothes and throw them on the ground. The soldiers warned that if the boys made any move they would be shot. My son Muhammad said, "Mother, I am too ashamed to take my clothes off in front of women." I told him, "Son, this is our fate."

Near the Sahah, there was a body of a man with a white beard. He was lying dead on the ground, and tanks were rolling right over him. I couldn't recognize him.

My children, Farid and Ali clung to me tightly. They were shivering with fear. An Israeli bulldozer moved toward us, coming really close. The soldiers ordered us to go to the mosque. Beside the mosque there were six young men who were tied and blindfolded. Right next to the mosque there was a large pile of glass. The soldiers came and took my son Muhammad. His upper body was naked. My son has asthma and he was very scared. They sat him on the pile of glass. Then he started to cry, and he said, "Mother don't leave me!" Two big soldiers attacked him. More kids were brought and were ordered to lie down on the pile of glass. I swear to God, they were forced to lie on the pile of glass! A big soldier sat right on my son's back and put the M-16 right in his ear. My son closed his eyes and began praying. The big soldier said, "Do you want to be a martyr?" My son did not reply.

The soldiers ordered the women to go to the municipality building. We started walking toward the town. A woman from the Damaj family was an amputee, she was missing a leg. She was exhausted and thirsty, and she fell on the ground and fainted. There was no one there to help us, so we started pulling her with us. A Red Crescent ambulance passed by and saw the woman, so it backed up and came to help her. But the soldiers opened fire at the driver. Several women carried two handicapped children. A woman who had no children carried one of the girls on her back. The other child was being carried by two women, one holding her legs, and one cradling her body. We would rest every few meters until we reached the clinic. Several tanks were stopping a

Red Crescent ambulance, the soldiers told the driver of the ambulance to come and explain the army's orders in Arabic. The driver came and said, "They are asking you to remove your head scarves and to lift your arms in the air. Those with children must walk with their children, and those without must walk with women in groups of three." So, we did as they ordered.

As we began walking we saw that they were holding more than thirty young men, including a young man that I knew. He was tied up and thrown in with them. As I walked, I prayed for him and for the others. We arrived in the center of the town of Jenin. As we arrived, people started dispersing, and suddenly an airplane opened fire from above. At the same time a tank started shelling. Bullets were flying everywhere. They were hitting the house of Um Ali Samoudi, the mother of Ali Samoudi, the journalist. Ali's mother came running and she called on all of us to come inside. I told her, "The soldiers took my son." Me and the other women sat and wept. Each one had lost a son or a husband. Some women had their entire families buried under the rubble. It wasn't even safe where we were sitting, I didn't care. I was crying for my son. I didn't care about our house or our life's savings, only my son. Twenty-one days later, I went back to my house. I found the breakfast that I made for Muhammad still there, cold tea and biscuits. Everything in the house was destroyed.

There is still no news of Nawal's son, Muhammad.

Hala Irmilat

A thirty-year-old mother of three, Muhammad (7), Hazar (6) and Rami (4), Hala Muhammad Sadiq Irmilat is of medium height and dark complexion. She wears a simple dress and head scarf. She says that she struggles with nightmares every night and cries frequently and her children continue to ask about their father. Her house is partially destroyed from the Israeli shelling. But there she lives with her children. She has no source of income.

The Israeli army was everywhere in the camp. They surrounded our house from all directions. Hani, my stepson, came on Wednesday morning to tell his father that the army was in our neighborhood. He did not realize that the Israeli soldiers were on the top of the mosque, they opened fire and shot him immediately. Our house is not far from the mosque, barely one hundred meters. Hani was killed over here.

She points toward the entrance of the house.

My husband did not see Hani then, but I did. He was taken by an ambulance that came to rescue the nurse and her sister.

On Friday, our house came under fire. Shattering glass and explosions were everywhere. My husband was very distressed, he wanted to know what happened to the house. He spent many years of his life saving to build this house. He came crawling into the living room and found it full of glass shards. He came back to put some shoes on and returned to the living room. Barely one minute later I heard one bullet. He was calling to me. He called to me three times, "Hala, Hala, Hala . . ." His voice was different. It was the voice of someone who was hurting. I knew he was shot. I was with the kids in the bedroom, and he was still in the living room. I came running and the kids ran behind me. Once I stepped into the living room I found him still standing. He looked at me and he asked me what happened, he gestured with his hands as if he still did not know what had happened. I asked him, "What happened to you?" Then I saw the blood gushing out of his head. He opened his mouth to answer me but he couldn't muster one word. He tried to speak again, and blood gushed out of his mouth, from his nose, and more from his head. He fell down slowly. I gazed at him and then looked to my frightened children. I wasn't sure where he was hit because blood was coming from everywhere. He looked upon me and upon our children, and then he shook. I knew that he had died.

I would like to add that my husband's body stayed in the house for seven days. He was martyred on Friday, April 5, and his body was not allowed out of the house until late the following Thursday. I begged the Israelis soldiers to allow him to be buried but they refused. The children and I were trapped with him in the same room for the entire time. The children were too young to understand what happened to their father. I had to tell them that their father was still alive. When the kids would quarrel, they would try to wake him up to complain. Just five minutes before Attieh was killed he was playing with Rami, telling him, "Don't make noise, the army will hear you."

"If I'm quiet," Rami said, "will you bring me a bottle?" After his father was martyred, Rami kept trying to wake him up to get him his bottle. "Wake up, Daddy. Why did you lie to me? I need my bottle," he kept telling his father. Of course Rami is only four, and he was under the impression that his father was just sleeping.

Amani Hussein Abu al-Raab

Amani is a simple yet beautiful fifty-five-year-old woman wearing a traditional Palestinian dress. Her wrinkles suggest that she has aged beyond her years. She has a strong voice inflecting courage and patience. She lives in the Sahah, in a house that was completely destroyed during the Israeli invasion. Despite that the destruction of her house has made her family homeless, she still has hope that her children will someday have a better life. Her eyes constantly fill with tears as she speaks. She gave her testimony sitting on the ruins of her home.

We were in our house when the Israelis first attacked the camp. They shelled with missiles before entering. The missiles fell on our homes. One of them fell on our neighbor's house, Said Ayesha. When we realized that they were shelling everywhere we fled. We sought refuge in a neighbor's house that appeared sturdier, over there.

She points a block away from her home.

Several families stayed in that home, including the family of Um-Saed, and the family of Um-Jamal and several other families. We were fifty-six people in one house. We stayed there Friday. The soldiers entered the camp Saturday. They broke into every home. They searched from house to house to house. Someone told us that the soldiers were close by, so we locked the home and sat inside awaiting our fate.

The Israeli soldiers broke in. They took a young man named Hamdan and interrogated him and then they brought him back. The house we were in was still intact. The soldiers kept sneering at us from outside through the window and gesturing with their hands that they were going to slaughter us. Then they came back into the house and separated some of the people from the group. They tied their hands and left them in the house, ordering us not to untie them. The soldiers would leave and be gone for hours, but then come back. They used the house as a center. When one unit left another would come. We remained tied this way for nearly a week, until the following Saturday.

The next Saturday they arrested my son Muhammad. They threw him on the ground on his face and put him on a pile of glass. They dragged him and made him walk in front of them while they broke into other people's homes. They entered into the house of Yasser Abu Khorj. I fainted once that happened.

They stayed in the house of Abu Khorj for a whole night and continued to beat my son. Even now, the bruises are all over his head. Blood was gushing from all over. They told my son that they were going to send him back home the next day. My son told a commander of the unit, "The soldiers are beating me, there are over 40 of them." The commander told them not to beat him up, but once the commander left one angry soldier took all of the blankets in the house and covered him up. He was that way for over an hour. He kept screaming, "I am suffocating!" They kept him in that house for three days, abusing him and refusing to let him go.

Muhammad said, "I need to go back to my children." The soldiers said, "We still need you." They would take him to other peoples' homes to protect them while they broke in and destroyed everything. Finally, they let him come back. Some of the women looked from the window and cried, "Your son is back!" I was so happy I jumped off the stairs. I still don't know how I managed to jump. Our house was completely destroyed. Bulldozers just came and toppled the whole thing. It was a big house, the result of many years of very hard work. Um Ali was the one who told me that the house was gone. I felt that my heart was crushed with it.

Amani started gesturing toward the ruins, describing what was there before it was destroyed.

This is my son's mattress, and this is my grandson's toy car. We couldn't salvage anything except the clothes that we were wearing. We seek justice from God, to deliver us from Sharon. If it *were* merely our homes we lost, it wouldn't have been as bad. It was all the blood that was spilled. That will never be replaced. The great losses were some of those whom I saw dead: Abu Jandal, and the five people in Shaban's house.

Amani confirmed that she witnessed the extra judicial execution of the resistance leader Abu Jandal. She narrates what she saw:

I saw him being shot. They tied him up in the Sahah. They blindfolded

90

him and had him sitting on his knees. It was amazing that they shot him twice, and yet he did not fall, he remained on his knees. He had nothing supporting his back, yet he remained in that position. He was shot with a bullet here and over here.

She points to her forehead and to the back of her head.

Once they left I approached him. I said, "God Bless you, Abu Jandal, you have died a hero." I told the women in the neighborhood that there was a beautiful perfume coming from his body when he was martyred

She goes on to tell of the other executions she witnessed:

I have seen five other people killed in Khalid al-Sadi's house. They savagely killed them—I could not even recognize their faces. They looked as if they were not humans. There was blood everywhere. What have we done to deserve such a fate? This life is worthless.

Faisal Sareh

Faisal Hussein Abu Sareh is a tall, sturdy man, 44 years of age who has thick black hair and high spirits. He looks as if he prevailed over the events in Jenin. He speaks with power. He lives with his family of 14 in a rented house in Jenin. His house is located in the Sahah. His married son also lives with him in the same house.

The Israeli army was first positioned at the outskirts of the camp. They occupied all the mountains and the hills that surround Jenin. They were able to shoot inside the camp while they were on the top of the hills. They were watching closely what was happening inside the camp. They started attacking first with tanks and airplane missiles. They bombarded all over the camp. On the fourth day my family sought refuge at our neighbor's home, Abu Jamal Bakizi. An average of four to five missiles fell every couple of minutes. The tanks were trying to enter the camp but they could not, for the resistance was very strong. During the night we would hear the bulldozers roaring, homes crumbling, as Israelis tried to create additional routes for the tanks. We knew that they had made it to the Sahah. Some fighters came to the house we were in, telling us that the Israeli bulldozers were already all the way to Abu Omar's house, very close to us. They warned us so that we could flee. There were many bulldozers and we knew that they were destroying many houses. We were still at Abu Jamal's house. Every time a missile would fall, we would start guessing whose house was hit. I had a good view from the window so I was able to see many of the homes coming down. This continued until the eighth day of the invasion. Until then, our home was still not destroyed. I tried to check on our house but the soldiers caught me and arrested me. I was caught with other people. The soldiers ordered us to strip naked. They took us to Salem and kept us there for four days.

They asked me about my name, and I told them. I was interrogated by the Shin Beit, Israel's intelligence. "Are you the father of the suicide bomber who blew himself up in Afuleh?" they asked. (Faisal's son, Mustafa was killed when he blew himself up among a group of Israeli soldiers in the Israeli city of Afuleh. He was a member of the Islamic Jihad.) The officer asked me, "How many did he kill?"

"Fourteen soldiers," I said.

"Incorrect," he replied, "he killed nineteen."

Faisal Abu Sareh

He accused me of being rude, so I replied, "I'm just answering your questions."

"Fine," he said, "we will deport you to Lebanon."

"It's not your right to do that," I told him. "In your country, once your son is eighteen, he is responsible for his own actions."

Finally, they decided to expel me with hundreds of others to villages close to Jenin. They forbade us from coming back to the camp but I sneaked back in five days later. It was all over. All the houses were gone. The Israelis bulldozed some and blew up the others. My house was totally destroyed. They blew it up with dynamite because it was the house of Mustafa Faisal Abu Sareh, my son.

Saed Hamdan

Saed Muhammad Mahmud Hamdan (38) works as a clerk for the Ministry of Youth and Sports. He is married and has several children. He was living in a two-story building with his family and his mother when the invasion began. He is a tall young man with black hair and a bald spot in the front. Initially, he exudes power and resistance, but he is unable to hide his anxiety and stress, symptoms that have haunted him following the invasion. He is very eloquent, but sometimes gets angry unexpectedly as we experienced during the interview. His house is located in an area near the Sahah.

When the invasion began we were near the center of the camp. We refused to leave our home, despite the fact that tanks and soldiers had completely sealed the camp. It was around two o'clock in the morning, if I remember correctly, and it was a few days after the invasion that a missile fell near our house and shattered our windows. Part of a neighbor's house collapsed, so they ran into our house. They stayed with us until the next day, Friday. By that time, parts of our house were also destroyed. We all decided that it was time to go and seek other shelter, and chose Jamal al-Faris's home. We went there along with Abu Muhammad's family, and we brought along Um Ali and her nephews and nieces. There were fifty-three of us. Our youngest was a year-and-a-half and our oldest was sixty-five.

On Saturday, at six in the morning, the soldiers broke into the house. They were terrifying. One of the soldiers rushed in and grabbed a one-year-old boy, one of Um Ali's nephews.

"What do you think," touching the barrel of his gun to the baby's head, "should I kill him?"

"That is a small child," screamed the women, "let him go!"

"You are a camp of animals," said another soldier in broken Arabic, "you are not human beings!" He started shouting at the women and using vulgar language.

Then the soldiers gathered all the men and boys and took them to a nearby house, the house of Rida al-Faris. They gathered all of us in one room after they handcuffed us. They started shooting right above our heads, laughing. Half an hour later, they picked me from the group to be used as a human shield, saying, "You will open homes for us!" They made me walk in front of them. First I was ordered to open Muhammad al-Fayed's home. I tried, but it was locked, so they came and they set explosives near the door and blew it open. They pushed me in, demanding, "Search the rooms!" I checked, but no one was there. Then they stood beside a window. Using radios, they communicated with an airplane that was circling above. They were telling the airplanes which homes to hit. I implored them, saying I have a heart condition and could not go any longer. They took me back and handcuffed me again. Then they took my nephew to use him as a human shield. They took him around eleven in the morning and around two in the afternoon we heard him screaming, "They want to kill me, they want to kill me!" We screamed at them, "What has he done to you?" That's all that we could do.

My nephew later told us that they brought a propane tank and ordered him to sit on it, blindfolded. Pointing a gun at him, they threatened to blow him up. They did that for hours, asking him questions, bringing pictures of people they were looking for. Each time he would say, "I don't know this person." They would start beating him, mainly hitting him on the head. My nephew told them he was living in Jordan and did not know these people. They brought him back that evening, terrified and covered with blood.

We stayed in that house until Wednesday, when Israeli soldiers began ordering us on loudspeakers to give ourselves up and meet near the brick factory. We did not leave. They fired over twenty missiles into the Sahah, to scare the men into leaving. Two hours later, they started calling on women and children to leave and to gather in the United Nations school for girls. Some of us would not allow our families to leave, because we did not know what the soldiers would do to them. At that point, we decided to leave the house to which the soldiers brought us and go back to our families.

On Saturday April 13, at around ten o'clock in the morning we heard noise. There were thirty soldiers who stormed into the house. Others were in the neighborhood setting houses on fire. It seems that they heard the sounds of the children. The first soldier to storm in started shooting while screaming, "Terrorists! Terrorists!" I need to mention that the handcuffs were still on and it had been seven days. So we lifted our hands in the air, hoping that if they saw us this way they might stop shooting. Their commander asked us, "What are you doing here?" We told him that a unit of his army took us and handcuffed us on the sixth of the month, and said that if we left they would kill us. That's why we wouldn't leave, we were afraid that they would kill us. "But haven't you heard the loudspeakers?" he asked. I told him that we could not hear over the sound of the missiles.

They interrogated us one by one underneath the stairs of the house. If any person gave them an answer that they didn't like, they would start kicking him and punching him. They took someone named Muhammad Abu Sareh. He was the only one who didn't return. A few days later Muhammad came back, and he was in miserable condition. They had him sleeping in a two-foot by two-foot bathroom. They were playing some sort of a game, holding a gun to his head. We were happy that the missing boy had returned. We congratulated him and we felt like a whole family again. I felt that the strength of the people inside that house is what helped us survive. We worried about the fate of everyone and tried to help each other as much as possible. And we survived.

We knew that things were getting better when we saw cars from the Red Cross. We started coming out of the house. I went out to check on people. I found Muneer Wishahe. He was cut to pieces because Israeli bulldozers kept running over his body after he had been killed. We also found Muhammad Nawrasi, who was also gruesomely killed. I saw Abu Jandal handcuffed and murdered. The other men and I started collecting these bodies. We had to bury them in the backyard of Sheik Tayah's home because the Israelis would not allow ambulances to take the dead bodies. People slowly started emerging from their homes. Then I found Nidal Nubani in a hole the soldiers dug that was five meters deep. They threw him in, but did not cover him. I also discovered the bodies of Amjad and Majd al-Fayed and many others.

Here we are still living. What can I say but thank God for everything—good or bad. It was a very, very difficult time for us. I have lost my home and all of my possessions. All that I came out with is my pajamas. Even my pajamas were torn and covered with blood when I was searching for bodies. I had to borrow a pair of pants from a thirteen-year-old boy. I had to wear them to cover myself.

With our will and determination, we will survive. We will rebuild our houses. Our fathers and grandfathers that were expelled here in 1948 survived as well. I have faith that we will all start over again.

Jamal Hussein

*A forty-five-year-old father of 11 children, Jamal Muhammad
Kamil Hussein is very poor and unemployed. He is a very kind and
gentle man. His way of talking indicates that he has not received
a great deal of education. He is very humble and sensitive, and
he says that he has no hope for the future. He worked as a cheap
laborer in Israel prior to the Israeli invasion and was living in the
Hawashin neighborhood during the invasion.*

During the invasion and the massacre, I stayed in my house, despite
the fact that I had lived through prior invasions. There was so much
bombing and shelling from airplanes and tanks. When our house came
under fire, we moved to Abu Mahmud's. That was during the fifth day
of the invasion. I was very scared, so I carried my children and started
running because our house, among many others, was being targeted by
the airplanes. The Israelis did not care if there were people in the houses.
They targeted the entire camp. We felt that Abu Mahmud's house was a
bit safer since fewer shells fell there.

I stayed there for one day and on the second day a few wounded
were brought to the house. They were civilians including a young man,
Mahmud Huweiti, who, God knows, might be dead because he has been
missing since the massacre and people are still searching for his body.
He was wounded by shrapnel from an airplane's shelling. The bones
were sticking out of his leg and a young man came and tried to help him,
you know, primitive kind of help, with whatever was available, just to
clean the wound. They called the ambulance, but the soldiers wouldn't
allow medical workers in the camp. The people in the house kept calling
the ambulance every day to save the wounded or to collect the bodies of
those who were martyred, but the occupation forces refused to let them.
It was so difficult for people because if you would even stick your head
out of the window, they would aim to shoot you. Israeli snipers were
occupying every high building and they were shooting everything that
moved. Several days later, I decided to leave that house. Abu Mahmud's
house was now under fire too. A miracle happened when a missile came
right through the window and exploded in a room that was empty. Some
of us had just been there, and we would have all died if we had remained
in that room. Abu Mahmud's house was used as a place for the wounded

to be gathered because there were two young men with some basic knowledge of medicine who were doing their best to help. All kinds of civilians were brought in, wounded women and young girls, some without an arm. Some were being pulled in covered in blood. I had to leave. I felt like it was inappropriate for us to stay. It was the best thing for those who knew something about first aid to stay in peoples' homes and to treat the wounded with whatever means possible.

The second house I moved to was the home of Abu Ahmed Shabrawi. Shortly thereafter, the airplanes began shelling that neighborhood too. They destroyed the home of Hatem Rakh. The roof of the house came tumbling down and the family was barely able to escape. They all rushed to the house we were in. I was there with my family, thirteen of us, and my neighbor had his entire family too. Some other people from the neighborhood also gathered there. We were fifty to sixty people in one home. We had no fighters with us, only civilians. The bullets made holes in the ceiling and in the walls of the house. All of us started jumping out of the windows. Whoever couldn't jump out was wounded. I held my children and we ran to the house of Yahya Shabrawi, located in a neighborhood called Jabriat. Yahya's house was a bit safer, but an hour later bulldozers moved in and began demolishing homes with people inside. People started running randomly, others died under the rubble. We stayed at Yahya's house for a whole night.

A shell hit the neighbor's house and it burst into flames. If one of these shells had fallen on the house we were in, more than a hundred would have been killed and wounded. The children were screaming all night and the adults were praying and reciting Quran. I was holding onto four of my children at all times, keeping my ears open for the airplane, so I would know when and where to run. At midnight, I decided to flee. Some people said, "Are you crazy, the snipers are all over the neighborhood, they will kill you if they find you out, go inside and read Quran and pray for God to protect you." So, I proclaimed, "There is no God but Allah and Muhammad is the Prophet of Allah," knowing that it was time to die. We remained in that house until the morning. When Shaul Mofaz, the head of the Israeli army arrived at the camp to supervise the army's invasion, they intensified the bombing. More than sixty missiles fell in a very short period of time.

Now the house we were in was severely damaged. The walls were about to collapse. So we decided to go back to Abu Ahmed Shabrawi's house. Once we got there, the bulldozer thundered up to it and immediately started demolishing the house. Loudspeakers were then calling on people to exit their homes. I told the people who were with us, "Let us exit with a white flag, otherwise we will be buried under the rubble." Some people said that if we stepped out, the snipers would immediately open fire. I said that whatever God willed would be. We made a white flag and left the house, all of us, with the women and children. I carried my son, and put my daughter on my back, and carried a third son. We came to an area that was completely bulldozed. The soldiers that were there started shooting right above our heads. They said, "Sit down or you will all die." We were terrified. Some women held onto their husbands; we knew that they were going to kill us. The soldiers said, "Women can go but all the men are going to die."

Soldiers stationed on the top of a nearby house started throwing dirt on us. The women were allowed to pass and fifteen men and boys remained. Half an hour later, a tank came and stood near us. They pointed the cannon at us. They spent over an hour terrifying us that way. The commander of that unit spoke in Arabic to us, "Go to the Sahah." While we were on our way, we kept reciting Quran. We felt that they were going to execute us. Once we arrived in the Sahah, we found a large number of men who had been forced to strip completely naked. There was a big pile of clothes. Soldiers started shooting right above our heads. They would call on us one by one. And once they pointed at you, you would have to pull your pants down and your shirt up. When it was my turn, I stood up and saw the body of a man, Jamal Sabbagh. It was some sort of a test. If you passed, you were arrested. And if you didn't, they would shoot and kill you.

We stayed there for five hours, handcuffed, under the blazing sun. I felt that I was dying from thirst. They had us walk in a long line, handcuffed and tied to one another. We walked for several miles behind a tank until we arrived at a village called Kufr Dan. Some of the people were arrested there and taken away. One of the commanders stepped up and said, "People who are forty-nine and above, you can go, under that age will have to stay." I noticed that some of the men with us were wounded and bleeding. I said, "I am in my fifties." The soldiers said, "You can go, but don't you dare ever go back to your refugee camp." We walked toward the valley, separating us from the village. We left the others behind, but days later we returned to Jenin anyway.

101

Hussein Jabali

Hussein Rajih Mifleh Jabali looks much older than the fifty-seven-year-old he is. He has white hair. His face is filled with wrinkles. He said that he did not have access to water to wash for twenty days during the invasion. He appears constantly nervous and heavy-hearted. He owned a shop that sold copper and was located in the same building that housed his family. That house is located in the Sahah neighborhood.

A few days after the invasion began, a large number of Israeli soldiers took over our house. They entered through the backyard and knocked on the window. I said, "Who's there?" No one answered. Suddenly, they all rushed in. They started shooting at the walls. They spoke in Hebrew. I had no idea what they were saying. One of the soldiers raised his hands in the air, gesturing for us to do the same. I raised my hands. He started shouting at me in Hebrew. Meanwhile the shelling in the neighborhood continued. Every time we heard an explosion, we felt it was all over.

The soldiers remained for hours. They locked the children in the kitchen and took me with them to the upper floor. They had me stand right at the window. They began clashing with resistance fighters, using me as their shield. I was so terrified. I felt I was going to die. I knew that getting shot was unavoidable, so I threw myself on the floor. One of the soldiers called me and he said, "Go to the kitchen. You stay there until the morning." They had me handcuffed and sitting in a very uncomfortable position. I didn't realize they were gone. My wrists were hurting very much and I really wanted to have a smoke. I also needed to go to the bathroom very badly. Finally I started knocking on the door and started calling, "Soldier! Soldier!" I managed to reach the knob of the door. I realized that it wasn't locked as I'd assumed, but I worried that if I opened the door and appeared to them suddenly, they would kill me. So I opened the door while continuing to call, "Soldier! Soldier!"

Then I went down the stairs and realized that the soldiers were gone. They left without untying us. It was around midnight and my children were also trapped. On the following day the soldiers came back, saying, "You better leave your house." As we left, soldiers stationed on the top of Abu Ali Eowese's house ordered us to come to them. One of the soldiers said, "Hey you, with the *kaffiah*. You take this body and put it in

Hussein Rajih Mifleh Jabali

your house."

"Yes, sir," I answered. They ordered two other people to bring the martyr and set him in front of my house. "But sir," I said, "I have children, they will be terrified, can I put him in my shop instead?" He said, "Fine, put it in the shop." But as I tried to open the door of the shop, it wouldn't open. Someone suggested that we put him in Massoud al-Wahdan's shop. We carried him there and we spent some time making a place for him. The martyr was covered. As I laid him down inside the shop I uncovered his face. He was from the al-Sabbagh family.

Israeli bulldozers have demolished my entire house. They left nothing. I came back and I am trying to start all over again.

Fyrial Jaber

Fyrial Khaled Abu Jaber, who is only 8 years old, talks with a very frightened tone. Her family said that she doesn't sleep well at night because she constantly has nightmares. She wets her bed every night. She used to do well in school but this is no longer the case, now she doesn't like school because she thinks that her school is going to be shelled at any moment. She is has a broken voice and hardly smiles. She constantly talks about how the soldiers broke her toys and tore up her books.

We were in the house. The soldiers came and started shouting, "Open the door!" We came to open the door, but the soldiers detonated it. The soldiers took my father and had him walk in front of them as they searched the house, and they took him to search another house. I was scared, I cried. They started destroying everything in our home: the vases, the television, and my doll. Her name was Ala.

Muhammad Amer

Muhammad Ahmed Muhammad Amer is a twenty-seven-year-old single man who worked as a cheap laborer in Israel prior to the invasion. He has a strong personality and loves to talk. But he re-lives very painful moments every time he attempts to recall the attack. He became very nervous and anxious when recalling the moment he saw dead bodies and cut our interview short. He lives in the Masjid Abdullah Azzam neighborhood, located on the west side of Jenin.

During the invasion, airplanes came and started shelling the Abdullah Azzam mosque. On the third day the mosque was severely damaged. Later, Israeli soldiers entered our neighborhood. They were placing dynamite on many doors and blowing them open.

The Israelis entered our home and they started breaking everything, on about the seventh day of the invasion. "If someone tries to enter your house and you warn him that there are soldiers here," their commander threatened, "we will blow you up." They took positions inside the house and waited. We were almost thirty people inside one room. We heard them wrecking and destroying. They destroyed all of our possessions. We were trapped in that room for two days with no food. When the soldiers left, we went out to check the rest of the house. We found everything destroyed.

I went down to the Sahah and I found five bodies, some decomposed. In a house in the Sumran neighborhood, I found several bodies in one room. I also saw some bodies being brought out from under the rubble. When I went to the school, I also saw many bodies. One was of a very old man, and . . .

Muhammad could not continue.

Ahmed Khalifeh

Ahmed Khaled Saed Abu Khalifeh (12) stopped telling his story when he began weeping. He cried for over an hour. His mother asked us to stop the interview. She said that he cannot sleep at night because he is so terrified. He doesn't spend time playing anymore and he isolates himself. He listens to the news a lot, and national songs. He doesn't like to hear the word "Israelis."

The first and the second day were okay. On the third day, I was looking out from the window of my house, and started calling on my uncle Mahmud. "Come and stay with us," I kept telling him. "I will," he said. But he never came. He was killed after that.

On the fourth day, missiles began falling on the Damaj neighborhood. We all ran to the basement. We could hear the sounds of tanks and soldiers talking and shouting. They started pounding on the front door and someone else was knocking on the back door. It sounded like one of my uncles. He was my uncle Juma. My father opened the door for him, but my uncle wasn't there. There was a line of blood on the ground. My dad went out to look for him. He found him sitting in the corner bleeding. He pulled him inside. The soldiers were now screaming at the door, ordering us to open. But we wouldn't because my wounded uncle was there. So, they blew up the door. They set us all in one corner and snatched my father. They had our neighbor walk in front of them, but then they left our neighbor and took my father.

Hussein Hammad

Hussein Muhammad Mahmud Hammad (45) has a family of eight. He cut the interview short when he began to weep, unable to continue. He was convinced that the camp was the victim of a conspiracy to destroy all of Jenin. He is also convinced that neither history nor newspaper reports will bring justice back to his camp. He speaks violently. He spends most of his time praying and reading Quran. The images of the massacre, he says, never escape his memory.

What I have seen are crimes; something greater than an earthquake. I have seen constant shelling from the air and the ground, snipers shooting and soldiers executing. What can I say? How can I describe this? The Nazis that they keep talking about were nothing like this. Many years of my life I have spent building my house. I put a brick upon a brick. I saved every penny to build a three-story home to host my entire family and their children one day. It all came tumbling down in a few seconds. I have no weapons. I have nothing. I could not defend myself, nor my children.

They came in hoards from the mountains, and then the fields, and in all directions. They called upon people with loudspeakers. First they called on fighters to give themselves up. We did not leave because we were not fighters. But then we thought, if we leave with or without weapons we will be killed anyway. We were only armed with the will of God. Only the angels stood by us.

The Israelis wouldn't let ambulances or any humanitarian relief reach the camp. The only treatment we had for the injured was to wrap their wounds in torn sheets or towels. During one incident, I was carrying an old man, Sheikh Riyad Badeer from Tulkarm. Sheikh Riyad is in his late fifties. He is one of the fighters and leaders of the Islamic Jihad. Despite the fact that he lives in Tulkarm, he came to the Jenin refugee camp to help defend the camp. He sold a small piece of land, all that he owned, and he bought light weapons to help the resistance. He came here and fought with our fighters. God bless his soul, he came to defend us. He was shot in the knee. I carried him on my back. I ran throughout the camp, begging people and screaming, "Please open your door to help this wounded man!" If anyone tried to open their door, snipers would immediately start shooting at them. So, I kept running around with him on my back like a madman. Missiles were exploding all around me. I finally asked him, "Where shall I put you?" He said, "Take me back to where I was wounded." I left him there. I came a few days later, it was still during the invasion. He was lying there, dead.

Maha Khorj

Maha Hassan Abu Khorj is a married twenty-five-year-old with four children: Hadeel (7), Hassan (4), Mahdi (2), and a nine month-old baby girl. Maha is a very simple woman, with beautiful black eyes. She is short and thin, very strong and eloquent. Her mother-in-law was present during this testimony. She interrupted Maha frequently.

I live on the third floor of a three-story building, located in the center of the camp, opposite the Hawashin neighborhood. During the invasion, my husband, my four children, and I went to my father-in-law's home. My husband Nidal is a shoe salesman. He is thirty years old. He was very nervous and he was extremely worried about the children. During the first day of the invasion, the electricity was cut off. We had to go to my father-in-law's home because our house is located beside a main street, and it was often an active route for Israeli tanks.

From the very first hour, people began talking about martyrs falling during the shelling. In the first few days the army failed to control the outskirts of the camp. But, the situation worsened when the army was able to make it into the camp. They blocked medical aid workers and ambulances from reaching the wounded. So whoever became wounded would die, even from a treatable wound. The bulldozers were brought in. The soldiers appeared savage, they made no distinction between woman, child or anybody.

They shot everywhere and missiles fell on the camp randomly. We had a very difficult time. First, we went with our children to my father-in-law's house, and from there, to my brother-in-law Waleed's house. The reason we went to Waleed's home was because my father-in-law's neighborhood was under heavy fire. The *shebab* were present in that area, and they were strongly defending that neighborhood against the advancing tanks. But even Waleed's house was no longer safe when the shelling moved that direction also. We decided to move to the Hawashin neighborhood because it was safer. At that time, the Hawashin was quiet, but at night the airplanes targeted that area with missiles. We were thirty people in one home.

The next day, the Hawashin neighborhood was severely attacked. We were terrified by the scene of the falling buildings and shattered glass. We kept running from one place to the other, all thirty of us. Shrapnel covered the streets. I would look to the faces of my children and see them almost yellow with fear. At a certain point, all thirty of us gathered in front of the bathroom in a small corner, barely a few meters long and wide. We were reading Quran while clinging to our children.

The adults pretended that they were not scared to comfort the fear of the children. My brother-in-law said, "The house is going to fall any minute!" He left on his own and sat under the staircase of another building at a neighboring house. That night we didn't go to sleep because the shelling did not stop at all. Around five in the morning the next day, a few people were in the neighborhood. We felt a sense of comfort so we too went out. Someone came running, shouting, "A tank is coming this way!" We ran terrified, and entered the house. Just five minutes after we entered my brother-in-law's house, an Israeli missile hit my house, which was just down the street. In my home, I live on the third floor and on the lower floors, there was the house of Mufid my cousin, and a room where my aunt Yusrah lived.

Yusrah is around sixty years old, and she is mentally handicapped. She doesn't fear the army at all. She would walk beside a tank if we let go of her. She would just go roaming the streets. She was in her room, standing in front of the window and a missile hit her. I wanted to go outside and check but people told me, "Go back in, the army will kill you!" But I didn't listen, I ran to my house. When I arrived a neighbor said, "The missile split your house from the middle and it is unlikely that your aunt Yusrah is still alive." I could not reach the house because the army was very close.

It was five days after that incident took place that we realized that Yusrah was martyred. On the fifth day, Israeli soldiers stormed into my brother-in-law's house. My brother-in-law begged them just to go and check on Auntie Yusrah. The soldiers said, "You have a few minutes to see if she is alive or not." He ran to our house and found her dead. The soldiers accompanied him on his way. She was hunched over, holding a blanket around herself. My brother-in-law asked to take her body, but the soldiers would not allow him.

We had no idea what was happening in the camp. We had no electricity or news. All that we knew was what we could hear, bulldozers demolishing homes, missiles landing. Toward the last days of the invasion, the soldiers ordered us out of our homes. As I left with my family, I found a man in his fifties. The Israeli army stripped him naked and had him stand in the sun. His skin was severely burned by the sun. I also saw a man who was an amputee. He was also stripped naked and sitting in the sun. There was a young man who was wounded and tied up, flies were all over his wound. The young man was bleeding, and yet they stripped him naked. On our way out of the camp, the young man tried to warn us about the soldiers, but they saw him warning us and began to beat him mercilessly. They grabbed his head and smashed it into the wall.

I still sit and cry when I look at my camp. Although living in a refugee camp is not the best life, it has been my home. Just seeing the way it looks now breaks my heart. Those days during the invasion were the hardest times of my life. Not one woman, man, or child did not cry during the invasion. After the invasion, I spent one week outside the camp, but I couldn't stand it anymore. I decided to come back one week later to check on my home and my aunt Yusrah. I snuck into the camp and I stood at the front step of my home. I found her in the corner of her room, covered with blankets, rocks were all over her. Although I think of myself as a strong willed person, I couldn't approach her. She was there for at least sixteen days. On the second day of my return to the camp, the curfew was lifted. My father-in-law and the *shebab* wrapped her in a blanket and put her in an ambulance. Her face was burned and she was dismembered. When we returned to our home, we found some pieces of her body and a few fingers still lying in her room.

Ibrahim Amer

Ibrahim Eid Amer's house is very humble and is located near the Jabriat neighborhood. He was wearing his pajamas and a small hat when we met with him. Despite the fact that his children were or are still imprisoned by the Israelis, he remains very defiant. Ibrahim (62) earns his living as a produce vendor. Ibrahim still appears to be in a state of shock, his thoughts are often scattered and difficult to understand.

It was after midnight when the invasion began. The Israeli army quickly took over our house and stayed there for ten days. On the second day, they made us move to the first floor, while they stayed on the second floor. I sat and listened to a radio program called, "The Arab's Voice." On the program, they announced that my son Ziad was martyred. I took my wife and we ran out of the house. We went to the hospital. As we entered the hospital, we realized others had been killed by Israeli snipers. Ziad my son was an officer in the Palestinian Preventative Security Forces. I was always worried about my son Ziad for many years. During the earlier uprising, Ziad was almost killed when Israeli soldiers opened fire at him and several other young men. Almost everyone was killed or wounded except for him. One day before this most recent massacre, Ziad came to my house and said, "Peace be on you, father." He said, "Could you please take my wife and stay in my home with my children?" He was wearing a shirt with a large spot of blood on the shoulder, it wasn't his blood. It was the blood of a wounded man that he rescued during an earlier invasion. He insisted on not washing away the blood. I remember joking with him because he had a big hole in his shoe. He said, "Dad, I don't know how you can find anything to joke about these days." I told him, "What else can we do?"

I had a dream earlier that while I was in my shop a woman came and she asked me for my red hat and my red *kaffiah*. I told her, "I need them, I am cold." She insisted until I gave them to her. When I woke up, I told my wife that the red hat was Ziad's blood and the red *kaffiah* was his coffin.

Just hours before he was killed, two of his brothers, one of them is also an officer, begged him to come home. They said, "Think of your wife and the future of your children." He told them not to worry and to

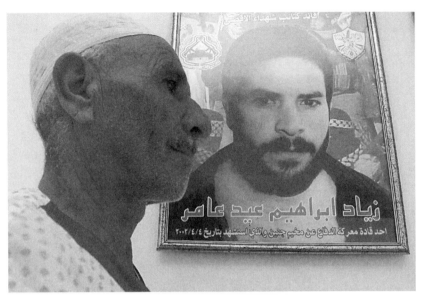

Ibrahim Eid Amer

go home to their families.

As they walked away, they saw an Israeli missile land on him and four of his comrades. My sons lost their minds when Ziad was killed. One of my children, Imad, is in prison for his role in the resistance. I cried for my son Ziad a lot. He was my firstborn and sweeter than all young men. I don't need money. I would give up everything just to have my son Ziad back. I still lie to his children, I take them food and tell them, "It's from your father." What else can I tell them? His wife is as helpless as me. She lost several members of her family during the invasion. She doesn't sleep at night. Her heart is broken.

Tufaha Tawalbe

Tufaha Tawalbe (47) has seven sons and two daughters. She is the mother of Mahmud Tawalbe, the leader of Al-Quds Brigade, the armed wing of the Islamic Jihad movement. Her husband is a produce vendor. Three of her children are in Israeli prisons.

After the invasion, Mahmud—may God be pleased with him—came to our house and said, "You need to leave, it is not safe here." So we left. Mahmud was twenty-four years old. He was involved with the resistance, making primitive weapons used against the Israeli army. Some of the weapons he made were used by resistance groups all over the West Bank. I kept telling him to stay away from these things. He used to say, "We have to resist, Mother. No one out there will fight this battle for us. We are the only ones who can win our freedom. I am not doing this for fame, for the sake of a person, or for money. I am doing it because it is the right thing to do." He used to visit us all the time. He would endanger his life, knowing that the Israelis were looking for him, just to come to kiss my hand and head. He would ask me to pray for him, and then he would leave. The last time I saw him was during the first days of the invasion.

The Palestinian Authority arrested Mahmud. He was arrested under the pressure of Israel and America. He was kidnapped from a street in Jenin. Thousands of people rushed to the street to protest his arrest. The Palestinian Authority then moved him to the Nablus prison, and he stayed there for seven months.

The Israelis tried to assassinate Mahmud on many occasions. One of these times, he was riding in a car with two fighters from Al-Aqsa Brigade. He stopped the car to purchase something from a pharmacy. At that moment the car blew up, and the two young men inside burned to death. Mahmud was wounded and was taken to the hospital. The Americans demanded that the Palestinian Authority arrest Mahmud from the hospital. Mahmud was hidden in a house in Jenin while recovering.

Around ten in the evening, many PA police cars came and surrounded the house. He was arrested. His arrest sparked anger in the streets. Protesters burned nine cars that belonged to the Palestinian Authority. This time he stayed in a Palestinian prison in Nablus for three months.

119

Tufaha Tawalbe

When I visited him in jail he told me, "Mother, I am afraid that they are going to poison me in jail." The Israelis then bombed the prison. Mahmud survived, however, he ran out barefoot. Celebrations erupted all over the West Bank because Mahmud survived.

When Mahmud wanted to get married he didn't tell me. He told his sister Maisoon. He was so sensitive and caring. He would even love a stranger. And he loved children so much. His wedding was in secret and no one was allowed there except for his other comrades—but I attended.

Mahmud had his second child Abdullah in March, just one month before the invasion. I brought Abdullah home from the hospital. I put him in a blanket and came searching for Mahmud all over the camp. When he learned that he had a son, he brought loads of candy and started giving it to everyone he saw. He was such a sweet son. He is the one who called his son "Abdullah" because he wanted him to be a servant for God.

When they attacked in April, he kept telling me, "Pray for me, mother." I felt he was not destined to be killed. He had survived numerous assassination attempts. Then I lost contact with him. It wasn't until I came back from the Red Crescent Center, when the invasion was over, that I learned what happened.

The rescuers found him in a friend's house, his friend's name was Abed. I was just returning from the center looking for my children and I was told to come and identify Mahmud's body. I refused to believe that he was killed. I looked at him, and I said, "No, this is not my son." But as I looked closer I said, "Yes, it is him." An ambulance immediately took him to be buried. I wish they kept him for a while, so that I could have held him. I still cannot believe that I will never see him again. I pray that I will see him in my dreams. But how, I don't know.

Mahmud's mother refused to wear black, as mourning women in the Palestinian culture often do. During Mahmud's funeral she told the women who were weeping to be glad because her son was a martyred hero. Her house was completely destroyed by Israeli bulldozers; she currently lives in a small rented house.

Samah Tawalbe

Samah Tawalbe is the twenty-four-year-old widow of Mahmud Tawalbe, the leader of Al-Quds Brigade, the armed wing of the Islamic Jihad movement. She is modestly dressed, wearing a simple long dress. She refuses to talk to the media. After a week of requesting an interview with her, she agreed. She said it would be the first and only interview she would ever give. Her voice is powerful and full of determination. She speaks about Mahmud as if she is talking about a legendary hero. Her children are constantly in her lap. She refuses to wear black because, for her, Mahmud's legacy has not died. She lives with her husband's family in a rented house, yet she has decided to use all of the money that she has received in donations following her husband's death to build a mosque in his honor.

When Mahmud first came asking for my hand I refused. But when he came and just talked to me, I changed my mind. We were engaged in 1996 and married in 1998. Mahmud was not wanted by the Israelis until the beginning of 2001, in the early months of the Intifada.

He was very sensitive, smart, and was kind to everybody. He never upset me, even for one day. When I gave birth to our second child Abdullah, Mahmud came to the house to kiss the baby. We sat and talked. He said, "Life is not everlasting, and it is eternity that counts." He was talking about Paradise, to the point that I told him, "You can't leave us, we need you." I believe he was aware of his fate. He said, "Do not worry, God will take care of you and the children if something happens to me."

He came one day before the invasion. He said, "Samah, the Israelis should be coming soon and they will be looking for me." He sat and prayed for his children. I told him, "Mahmud, you have never upset me and I have never upset you. I just want you to forgive me if I have done anything that I should not have done." So he started weeping. I felt like he didn't want to leave the house. I told him, "Mahmud, what are you waiting for? You must go before they come for you."

He left but came back twice that night. He never did this before, normally we hardly saw him once a week. I felt like he kept returning because he knew it would be the last time he would see us. He told me to leave the house. I told him, "No, I am staying." He insisted, so I took my children and I went to my brother-in-law's home. Then Mahmud, knowing that the Israelis would be coming to search and to destroy our house, detonated it so that they could not find anything.

He believed that we had no other choice but to fight. He often said that the Israelis should pull back to the 1967 borders, and if they would not we would keep on fighting. He once said, "Sharon is calling me a terrorist, but he is the terrorist. Isn't he the one who killed Iman Hajo* and Muhammad al-Dura* and hundreds of other innocents?" It was the killing of Muhammad al-Dura that angered him the most. He said, "Sharon will pay for this." He never feared death. He used to say, "Death is not in Sharon's hands, it is in God's hands." He used to say, "I would rather die in the battle for freedom than any other death." He used to pray that he would never be captured.

When I first learned that my husband was killed, I was very saddened. But then I decided to walk with my head held high. I didn't know if he'd died in the battle as he wished until a man who saw him in the last battle told me, "He died while fighting his enemies face to face." This man also told me that Mahmud was fasting and praying during most of the invasion.

The Israelis claim that Mahmud led the battle in the camp with five hundred fighters. But I know that there were barely fifty fighters. They fought with all the means they had to defend the camp.

My husband was very shy. He would talk to women with his eyes on the ground. He always took care of orphans, whether sons of martyrs or any others. For our honeymoon he took us on a pilgrimage to Mecca. I loved him so much. I used to tell him that nothing but death could separate us.

In the last battle, he refused advice to give himself up with all the other fighters. "The people of Jenin have stood by us and have supported us and I cannot abandon them in their hour of need." Mahmud told the fighters, "Whomever wants to give himself up can do so." This is what one of the survivors told me in a telephone call from the Askelon prison. The prisoner also told me that Mahmud died in a battle in Abu Jawad's house, in the Hawashin neighborhood. His face was completely burned. The people loved him so much."I will not believe that he died until I see him," I told him.

During the invasion, a house caught on fire with the people inside.

Mahmud left his comrades and jumped in the fire saving the people inside. This was in the Damaj neighborhood. He spent some of his time moving from house to house, distributing whatever food he was able to find. A woman gave birth in her house during the invasion and the father asked Mahmud to name their baby girl. He said, "Name her Sumoud, (Arabic for "resistance") because we will resist to the end." He was so proud of the battle he and his comrades were able to fight to defend our refugee camp. I found the hat he was wearing in the house where he was killed. I took the hat to give it to our son. When he grows up I will tell him that his father was a hero and I am very proud of him.

I told Mahmud that nothing would separate us but death and I will tell my children the same. Since Mahmud's death, my faith in God has grown tremendously. Mahmud was a great leader and the people loved him. He was so kind to them. He used to give away the last bits of food and water we had in the house. If I would make a comment about a beautiful house and say, "Look at this beautiful house," he would say, "Eternity is more beautiful." Now I make my children wear green pajamas, because he used to say that Paradise is green. He was very, very humble, and always asked me to be humble.

Iman Hajo, a four-month-old infant from Khan Yunis, was killed when an Israeli tank shell struck her home on May , 2001.
Muhammad al-Dura, a twelve-year-old boy from Buriej refugee camp in the Gaza Strip, was killed by Israeli fire on September 30, 2000.

Um Nasser

Um Nasser means mother of Nasser and is how friends address Karima Abdullah Abu Hatab. She is sixty years old and has a family of eleven. Her house is very simple and sparsely furnished. They had no chairs so they had to borrow a few plastic chairs from a neighbor's house to conduct this interview. Um Nasser wears a very simple long dress. She is dark and her eyes are hollow. She appears to be weary and overwhelmed with sorrow. During our interview she shifted between weeping and talking.

In the first days of the invasion, the Israelis could not enter the camp. But they shelled from outside. One shell landed in our living room. My husband, who is an old man, was wounded in both his legs. My son Nasser was not home, but he knew that our house was hit. He was very worried so he came running with some of his comrades into the house. He came amid the shelling and had Mahmud Tawalbe also with him. If it wasn't for them we would have died in the fire. They carried me and my husband and helped us escape from the back of the house.

Some of the *shebab* were distracting the soldiers to make safe passage for us. Our family was running all over the place and Nasser's three children ran to the neighbor's home. We went to Um Samed's house, a neighbor of ours, but the Israelis started shelling her house too. The *shebab* took my husband and helped us escape elsewhere.

Because they came to rescue us, the *shebab* had revealed their positions. An Israeli airplane kept chasing after them from one house to the other. Finally, the *shebab* left my husband in front of a house where forty people were seeking refuge. They were all gathered in a small basement. My husband was screaming in pain and said he could not go down the stairs, so he stayed on the first floor. The second floor of that house was destroyed. Three missiles struck it and part of the house caught on fire. We managed to survive and we stayed at that house for two more days. We knew nothing about Nasser and his comrades.

These were some tough days. We were running for our lives from one spot to the other. My husband's wound was very painful and it hadn't been checked for days. One of my daughters told me she couldn't stand not knowing what happened to her brother Nasser. She said she wanted to sneak out to check on the house and to see where Nasser went. After she jumped out of the window, she found Nasser lying dead. She came back sobbing, telling me, "Mother, they shot him in the face."

My son and our neighbor's son took blankets and snuck back to cover him. They found that Nasser was also shot in the stomach. It seems to me that when they first shot him in the head they were not sure whether he was dead, so they shot him again. He was lying there for several days without us knowing. As soon as the curfew was lifted Nasser's four brothers wrapped him in a blanket and took him to another area before the Israelis could get a hold of him. As they were on their way out, they saw Israeli tanks approaching. Luckily an ambulance with two other bodies was near. The driver told them to leave Nasser's body with him and he would secure his burial. What can I say, besides God bless his soul and the souls of all of those who were killed. How can we forget these days? I still shiver with fear and anger when I remember them.

Um Siri

Um Siri has a family of five. She is very generous and has a sense of humor. She is 45 years old and wears a simple dress and a head scarf. She appears very strong and very patient.

Initially we thought that this invasion would be like other ones; that they would shell from the outside, enter for a day or so, and then leave. But it was nothing like that. Shells and bullets were like rain. My son refused to leave the house behind, although the shelling was very close. He said, "I still do not forgive grandfather for leaving Palestine in 1948, I will not commit the same mistake." On the first day, our house was still spared by the shelling but the second day was a disaster. It began at night. The house was shelled and some of its walls came tumbling down. We started crawling on our hands and knees as the shells fell all around us. We started reading Quran and prayed for God to protect us.

At that moment, I had been making some food for the *shebab* who were defending us from the Israeli army. They were near our house when the shells began falling. I started screaming for help. Raed and Mahmud Tawalbe, along with two others from the resistance risked their lives to save us. Raed carried my mother and we ran into a neighbor's house. My son was in his pajamas. The neighbor lady brought some mattresses for us to sit on. My son said, "I have to go back to get my ID." But one of the *shebab* said, "Don't worry, I'll get it for you." I told him to go and to take out all the food and give it to the *shebab*. During those days, I used to say, "God bless you," to the resistance. They had so much will and courage.

Now, the house we were seeking shelter in also came under attack. It was the home of the Saadi family. An old woman, Um Al-Abed Saadi was praying when the glass shattered and struck her in the back. We started screaming, "Get the ambulance!" She said, "I'm not going anywhere, I will die in my home." The *shebab* then escorted my family and the neighbor's family to another house. As we left, my two girls became afraid because of the bullets flying all around us and ended up leaving with the neighbors while my son, my mother, and I escaped into a different house. There we found twenty-five other people. The owner of the house welcomed us and escorted my mother into a special room, but soon their house was under fire too. Parts of their house collapsed and the glass in the windows shattered.

We stayed until sunset, when we heard muttering outside. Looking out the window, the house owner said, "It's the Israeli soldiers, it seems that they have been surrounded by fighters." The trapped soldiers began shelling homes to clear a safe passage for themselves. They bombed Abu Ghareeb's house, they leveled some of the walls and now they had access to the street. At around eight or nine in the evening, they also bombed Abu Abdullah's and Abu Nizar's homes, all of which were partially destroyed.

At nine in the evening, someone knocked at the door. We thought it was the soldiers. The owner of the house opened the door and told us, "Do not worry, it is Abu Jandal, a leader from the resistance." Abu Jandal told the owner of the house that eight Israeli soldiers had been surrounded and the *shebab* needed to go to the second floor of his house to close them in. The owner of the house apologized, saying, "We are twenty-six people in this house, and Israelis are murdering civilians for no reason, so I cannot let you in." Abu Jandal said, "I would never do anything to harm you. In fact, all we are doing is trying to protect as many of our people as possible." He wished us safety and left.

We spent that night praying that God would give us more strength and determination to survive this. We prayed for the *shebab*. We trusted them because they fought for an honorable cause. Of course a gun cannot stand before a tank, but we had faith in them. The next day around noon, there was no electricity, no telephone, nothing. I was talking with my daughters who were trapped in a different house when the phone line went dead. News came to me that my brother was shot and arrested by the soldiers. He was twenty-two years old.

Soon after, the Israelis came and knocked at the door. The owner of the house cried, "Do not detonate the door, I have children and women in here, I will open it for you." He opened the door and they dashed in like animals. They told him to shut up and the kids in the house, ages fourteen to fifteen all gave themselves up. The soldiers took the owner of the house and started punching him in the mouth. They asked him, "Where are the fighters?" He said, "I don't know." His denial only made them angrier, so they forced him to the ground and they stepped on his face. The soldiers had him stand up against a wall and they started firing their guns between his legs. Then they took my son, they had him strip naked and they also started firing between his legs to terrorize him.

130

I held my mother, she was ninety. The Israeli soldiers started rounding up women and they forced me and my mother outside the house. My mother was barefoot and there was so much shattered glass outside the door. They forced her to walk on the glass. Her feet started to bleed. They also rounded up the men and children. They gathered them in Abu Nizar's half-destroyed house. They handcuffed and blindfolded them and took them to the second floor. They rounded up more men and boys and interrogated them for the rest of the day and the whole night. They were beating them up constantly.

I pleaded to them, I said, "Where are you expecting us to go? I have my ninety-year-old mother with me." A soldier told me, "Stay here, just for half an hour. We have taken over the camp, the war is over." So, I sat with my mother. She kept asking me where we were. The soldiers kept looking at us in a way that terrified us. My mother was muttering some prayers, every time she did so, the soldiers would say in broken Arabic, "Damn your God!"

The next morning, I begged them for a drink of water for my mother. They told me they had no water, yet they were drinking in front of us, the liars. They locked us in a room, I started weeping and shouting, "For God's sake, open the door!" I told them, "Don't you say in the media that

Um Siri

131

you treat women and children humanely?" Someone opened the door and asked me my name. I changed my name, I had to, I told them my name was Mariam Abu Shenab. The soldier asked me in broken Arabic if I spoke Hebrew. I said, "No." He said, "So what do you speak?" I responded, "Only Arabic." So, he started cursing Arabs, our religions, and where we came from. One of them commanded me, "Shout at the top of your voice 'Long live Sharon!'" I said, "Why won't you leave me alone?" But he insisted, so I screamed, "Long live Sharon."

Every time an old woman would cough, they would start screaming at her and cursing. Every time an old woman would pray, they would do the same. My mother told me that she remembered when the English colonized Palestine, they were not as savage as the Israelis, she said.

Three soldiers stormed the room. They said, "Where are the cell phones?" I told them we had none. They looked angry and vicious. There were a few necklaces and watches that belonged to the owners of that house. I went and I snatched them before the soldiers got to them.

My mother extended her arm, trying to reach some water and all three of them attacked her. They started punching her in the chest. I screamed at the top of my lungs for them to stop, I threw myself at my mother and wept, "My mother, my dear one, they are killing you!" One soldier started pounding on my shoulder and another started stepping on my leg. They snarled obscenities at me, things I cannot say. They beat my mother for wanting a drink of water. I laid my mother's head on my shoulder and my mother fainted, not waking until two hours later. A soldier stepped in and said, "What are you crying about?"

"My mother was beaten by you soldiers," I said, "and we have no food or no water." I asked him if we could go to see a doctor. I was devastated, hungry, and thirsty from crying for my mother and my lost children. A soldier told me that I would be allowed to go, he said, "If you don't come back, we will kill you."

Once I stepped outside the door, I found the jacket of my son, the one he was wearing before they arrested him. It was sitting on the shattered glass, outside in the rain. Just seeing it made me start weeping again. "Where are my children, where are my children?" I kept saying. I took my mother and we walked down the street. We passed by the sons of Sheikh Abdel Salam. They were standing there in the rain, after the Israelis had them strip completely naked. There was a woman who was with us. She took her head scarf and tore it into several pieces so the young men could cover themselves.

A very thin old man approached while screaming, "My sons, my money, for God's sake, they took everything!" The Israelis had him strip naked like the day he was born. Once the women saw that, they started pulling their hair, hitting their heads and wailing. He had all of his life's savings with him, because he was worried that he might lose it in the invasion, but when the Israelis stripped him naked, they found the money and took it.

At that point, more people were ordered to leave the camp. I joined them. I took my mother to the hospital, but the Israelis were in control of that too. They ordered me to go back, so I went to another hospital. Nurses rushed and took my mother, gave us some water, and my mother IV fluids. There was some food left in the hospital, some bread and jam. We stayed there for several days, my mother was very sick. She couldn't go to the bathroom.

Eight days later, I went back to our house in the camp. I found it destroyed. There was blood in there. They smashed everything. They urinated on whatever food was there. I returned back to the hospital to be with my mother. Someone told me that my girls were in the Red Crescent Center. I went running. If you could see the situation we were in . . . I held onto my girls tightly and started crying. I couldn't believe they were still alive. I also found my son. He told me that the soldiers took him to a field near the camp with many other young men. He told me that the soldiers made them walk in front of the tanks while they were looking for fighters.

Just yesterday, as I went to the house that we rented after our home was destroyed, an Israeli tank chased me. What have I done to them? They have no respect for humanity. They do not distinguish between a child, a woman, or an elder. They cannot be trusted, they have massacred us for many years.

Um Siri's mother died a few days after this interview was conducted. She died from the injuries she sustained from the beating that Um Siri spoke of in her testimony.

The al-Shalabi Family

The al-Shalabi family has eight children, six boys and two girls. Most members of the family suffer from mental or physical disabilities. They live in a very small house. The following interview was taken with three family members: Yusuf, the father of the house, his daughter Seham, and his son Bilal.

Yusuf al-Shalabi: A few days after the Israeli army attacked the camp, they rounded up the women and men in our neighborhood and sent us to different destinations. I was walking near the clinic when the soldiers opened fire and hit me in the leg. I was taken to a nearby home to be treated. Later, the Israelis took me to a detention center and finally to the Jenin hospital. I remember this nightmare very well. It is very difficult to talk about it. I remember them stripping the people naked, handcuffing and blindfolding them. I remember seeing two wounded men, one was wounded in the shoulder, the other in the leg. They were screaming in pain and the soldiers would not allow them to be treated.

Seham al-Shalabi: I work as a tailor in a shop in the camp. Currently I am unemployed. The economic conditions are too difficult, and the shop couldn't continue. When the Israelis first entered the camp they came from the western neighborhood—our neighborhood. Most of the resistance was concentrated in that area. The resistance was very strong, led by Raed and Mahmud Tawalbe. In the first few days, the soldiers couldn't enter because of the resistance. It seems that the Israelis were not shooting bullets at our neighborhood, but rather fired shells randomly from tanks. The tanks were concentrated toward the mountains. They also shelled from the air. Abu Jandal was also in our neighborhood. He was a very courageous fighter. On one occasion the Israeli soldiers were trapped near Um Siri's house. They started shooting like crazy. We were in our house.

Two of my brothers are physically handicapped, they were terrified from the shelling, especially as it drew nearer. A missile landed on our neighbor's home, and another fell on the roof of another neighbor's home. It made a huge hole in the roof. My cousin and his son ran from their home to ours. We had very little food and water.

The soldiers knocked at our door, they came in, and broke down the door of my brother's room. They also took over Abu Muhammad al-

Badawi's house. Even now, he is still missing. God knows where he is; he might have been martyred.

Nearly eight days later the soldiers ordered all the people to leave their homes. They said that all of the homes would be destroyed. My uncle came, "They are going to shell us with F-16s," he said, "we have to escape." So we went outside. On the outskirts of the camp, Israeli soldiers separated men and women into different groups. They took all the men and boys. They made no distinction, even the mentally retarded, they had them stand in the sun. They made them take their clothes off and lie on the ground.

There was a young man who was wounded and bleeding from his shoulder. The ambulance stood by, trying to get to him, but the soldiers wouldn't let the ambulance near him. One of the women in our group was a nurse. She had some bandages and she wanted to go and help him but the soldiers shouted and threatened her, and so she went back. But we snuck the bandages to him anyway. They gathered all the women in a destroyed house. An army jeep came and started circling the house, then it opened fire at us. Why would they open fire at us? Then they came and they searched us and had us walk two by two, out of the camp.

Just as we began walking, we saw another group of tanks and bulldozers. We found some doctors and medical workers, stripped naked and handcuffed. Then they put them in trucks and took them to the Salem detention center.

The Israelis started shouting and ordering us to take off our scarfs. Some soldiers came and started pulling at our clothes. We walked until we reached Faisal Street. There was a tank that opened fire at us. We ran until we were in a safer area. I had no idea where my brothers were. They were six, some of them disabled. I later learned that they were in the Taibi, a small village near Jenin, and they were safe.

A few days later, we returned to the camp. The camp had been bulldozed. The scene is impossible to describe with words. Near the clinic, I saw a body that had been completely burned. Some people gathered the ashes and put them in a bag, the whole body could hardly weigh more than five kilos. The smell of death hovered over the entire camp. Some homes still had martyrs inside. I passed by my uncle's home and it was completely destroyed. The soldiers burned everything inside before they left. Our family was finally reunited nearly twelve days after the end of the invasion. One of my brothers who was left in a village named Rumana, roamed the area for days until he found us. My brothers Bilal, Jamal, and Ibrahim were detained for several days. They were left blindfolded and without any food, if they lifted their heads up, they were beaten. One of my brothers complained that the handcuffs were too tight. A soldier told him, "Let me loosen them a little." But he tightened them more. All of their hands were bleeding.

Bilal al-Shalabi: The soldiers took us from the camp to Salem. For two days, they had us sleeping on gravel, without food or water. We were handcuffed and blindfolded. Then around midnight we were dragged into another prison in Ramallah. The army bus made many stops. We

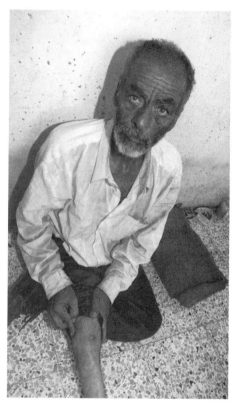

Yusuf al-Shalabi

were afraid that they were going to expel us to Gaza. We stayed in the new prison until three in the afternoon the next day. The soldiers took us and made us sit in the sun; it was a very warm day. One by one they took us to the interrogation room.

I saw Raed Tawalbe, the brother of Mahmud Tawalbe. The soldiers told him, "Your brother is dead." Raed would shout back, saying, "My brother was martyred!" The soldiers would shout back, saying, "No, he is dead!" But Raed kept saying, "My brother is a martyr." One soldier got mad and started punching Raed in the face. Raed was stripped naked. Each one of us faced several rounds of interrogation. A few days later, they let a few of us go but kept many.

I can never forget these days; the invasion and the detention. How could I forget my best friends, Nidal, Muhammad and others who were killed? I feel like my life is empty.

Aeshi Turkman

Aeshi Ahmed Turkman is an elderly woman unsure of her exact age who lives in a very small yet very organized house. She is tall, dark, and has a strong voice. She appears healthy and strong willed. She has seven sons and five daughters. One of her sons, Lutfi, was killed by the Israelis during the first uprising in the late 1980s.

One day before the invasion, I left the camp. I wasn't running away but I wanted to escort my two sons, Basem and Sael, who are handicapped to my sister's home. On the fourth day of the invasion, my son Muhammad was wounded by shrapnel from a missile fired by the Israelis. Doctor Waleed Nasharti tried to treat him but could not get him to the hospital. The Israelis would not allow any ambulances in or out of the area. Instead, my son was taken to Abu Mahmud's house, and he stayed there for nine days. The Israelis then stormed the house, took Muhammad and put him in a tank and left. Since then, I have been trying to find my son. After days of constant searching, the Israelis told us that my son was in an Israeli hospital. They said they would give me a final answer regarding his fate the next day. Later they denied that he was there. A relative of ours said that he saw Muhammad on Israeli

Aeshi Ahmed Turkman's daughter holding a photo of her deceased brother.

television, being carried by two soldiers. Why are they denying me the right to know what happened to my son? Do they just want me to die from bitterness and worry?

There is a God, and I have faith in him. My heart tells me that my son is still alive. I believe in God, not in Israel.

Abu Fathi

To friends Raja Mustafa Abu Aeta is known as Abu Fathi. Abu is 72 years old, is missing all his teeth and doesn't hear very well. He lost much of his hearing when the Israelis threw a sound bomb near his house. He lived through several wars. He witnessed the expulsion of Palestinians in 1948 and remembers the 1967 war in detail. He says what happened in Jenin was worse than anything he had ever witnessed. His house is tidy and he appears to be financially privileged compared to other refugees in the camp. He has many children and his oldest son Fathi is in an Israeli prison.

The *shebab* fought for two or three days but then were forced to retreat. The Israelis advanced into the camp after a few days of senseless bombing. My sons ran away an hour or two before the Israelis arrived. I refused to leave. "I will stay in my home," I vowed. I locked the house very well, but suddenly the Israelis started firing and they blew the door of my house right off. They stormed the house. I lifted my arms up in the air. One soldier threw a sound bomb at me. I had an old man taking refuge in my house. The man, Ahmed, is very old and has a hunch in his back. A soldier sat down and shot him. I cried out, "Why would you do this, he is an old man." They told me, "Mind your own business."

The soldiers divided themselves into two groups, one group searching the upper floor and one searching the lower floor. I looked at Ahmed and I saw a pool of blood. I knew he was dead. There were nearly thirty soldiers. They tied me up and then tied me to the couch. It was late at night, I asked them if I could have a cigarette or if I could go to the bathroom, but they refused. The next day they untied me. I looked around and I saw Ahmed my dear friend, also tied up even though he was dead. These people do not believe in God.

Then they used me as a human shield, they had me walk in front of them to four houses. At a certain point, "I am not going with you anymore," I said. One of the homes that they searched they completely destroyed. I pleaded to them to allow the ambulance to take the body of Ahmed.

Then they took me back home. There, I found fifty-seven-year-old Kassem Abeid. Kassem and I stayed there for two nights. We moved the body of my old friend into another room. The soldiers left and ordered us to stay, saying that they would be back. But we decided to escape. We snuck into a house nearby. The family was very welcoming. Then we managed to escape out of the camp. Although I am a man who has lived through so much hardship and have seen several wars, I could never forget what happened those days in Jenin.

Muhammad Rafi

Muhammad Rafi (35) works for the Red Crescent Society, heading up youth development programs. He has been working with the Red Crescent for fifteen years. He is very thin and has thick glasses. He is very humble with a quiet voice. The information he presents is very organized. He is very proud to be part of the team at the Red Crescent.

Volunteers in the Red Crescent have worked side by side with ambulance drivers to rescue as many lives as possible throughout the invasion. We managed to rescue wounded on the first and second days following the invasion. On the third day, we were allowed to do nothing. An Israeli tank came and parked right outside the gate of the Red Crescent Center. They did not allow anyone in or out. If one of us wanted to leave for the hospital across the street, it took two hours of telephone calls and deliberation.

Ambulance drivers with bleeding people inside their vehicles were forced to wait for two hours before they were allowed entry to the hospital. They took our volunteers or drivers, stripped them naked, interrogated, and insulted them. However, we refused to give up despite everything. Some of our volunteers were wounded and others, such as Muhammad Zidan, were arrested. Muhammad is still in an Israeli jail, although it was very clear from the way he dressed that he worked for us.

When people were forced out of the camp, they had no idea where to go. They were terrified. It was an incomprehensible moment. Some of them came running barefoot and gathered by the hundreds. They looked very sad and pitiful. If you tried to talk to any of them they would start weeping. They stayed for a while until they managed to find shelter elsewhere. Some stayed with relatives, and others managed to rent a room or two.

Our Palestinian brethren in Israel have stood with us, sending food and medicine. This is a gesture of the unity of Palestinian blood. I have worked for fifteen years for the Red Crescent, and this was the most difficult experience I have ever had. The terrorism and Nazi-like behavior of the Israeli army cannot be described with mere words. I was one of the first to enter Jenin once the Israeli army allowed entry. We had a Canadian expert who joined us. We felt like we were in an area that was struck by an earthquake. We saw bodies scattered all around us, and were instantly struck by the stench of death.

I find it difficult to recall these moments. The resistance was strong but what can one do before the Apache and F-16? Stubborn determination however is part of human nature. If you mistreat an animal, even an animal will defend himself. Why wouldn't a human being do the same as he finds himself facing death?

In the Center, we have done amazing things that make us very proud. I have worked very hard with others on the issue of those missing. We have cooperated with the Red Cross and various human rights groups. We have done all we could to collect news about people who have disappeared. You see, after they arrested so many people, some were killed and dumped in nearby villages. We have tried to keep the families updated on our findings.

We are also working on the issue of prisoners, along with the Red Cross and B'Tselem. We are trying our best to help the wounded. We've managed to find some people still alive under the rubble. We are working with others to clear the area of land mines left by the soldiers. There have been scores of people wounded by these land mines. A doctor who was helping us was wounded by a land mine and had his leg amputated. Two people were killed so far and many were wounded, some permanently disabled as a result. We worked with UNICEF in this field. We have assembled a team of volunteers and we have tried to educate the people of the danger of these explosives.

I am very proud to be working for the Red Crescent. The invasion was very shocking to all of us, especially to our volunteers who had to deal with the catastrophe in the camp once the soldiers left. They are in constant danger, harassed, insulted, beaten and detained. The psychological pressure is immense. But our volunteers insist on coming back, despite all that they endure. Their humanity is much greater than the hardships.

Um Ali Aweis

Um Ali Aweis is 50 years old and the mother of two sons and five daughters. She is one of those who did not leave the camp at any time during the invasion. She has a fair complexion and wears a traditional Palestinian dress. She said the saddest moment in her life was when she learned that the resistance surrendered. Her children gathered around her during this interview. One of her daughters is blind. Her husband is crippled, and must use crutches to move around.

When the Israeli army surrounded the camp on April 2, they could not penetrate it. They started building up more forces for five days and they were shelling and bombing from the sky. The resistance had few weapons that were very simple and primitive. It wasn't the strength of these weapons that made them stand the siege, but God and the angels who fought with them.

Our house is located in the Sahah. When the Israeli soldiers managed to find a way into the camp we were very scared. We were scared for our safety and the safety of the *shebab*. I was one of the few women activists who was daring enough to go outside during the attack. I used to prepare food for the resistance and deliver it to them.

The bodies I have seen in the streets are beyond description. The Israeli soldiers came to our house. They were very savage, hitting and punching and terrorizing everyone. They put us all in one room and then ordered us to leave the house. "Where will I go with my children?" I said. "You can topple the house on us if you want to, we are going nowhere. It's enough that you forced us to leave our homes in 1948, now you are even asking us to leave the refugee camp!" A soldier came up and punched me, and he called me an "animal!"

We slept that night. On the second day, around ten in the morning my niece was playing with a toy. It seemed that the resistance was fierce outside. The solders came and said, "All of you go to the upper floor." I said, "We are not going," because he wanted to use us as human shields. So he grabbed my niece and threw her under his arm and pointed a gun at her head.

"I will kill her if you don't go upstairs," he said. I came to take the child away from him, so he hit me on the head with the butt of his gun.

Um Ali Aweis

I had no choice but to obey his orders. Later I took my children and left the house. We went to a house that was a bit farther from the Sahah. Some people were already seeking shelter in that house. There were nearly sixty people in one home. I left my children there, took some food, and left the house, trying to smuggle the food to feed the *shebab*. I was relying on the help of God to protect me.

I have been wounded three times in the past. I consider all the *shebab* my children. They are putting their blood on the line to protect us. Our house was turned into a military barracks. The soldiers were there for nearly five days, and when they were finished with the house, they detonated it.

I was very close when they executed Jamal Sabbagh, a young man who was fighting with the resistance. They took one of our blankets from my home, wrapped him up and threw him in the street after they shot him. His body lay there for three days, and they ran over him with a tank

By that time we ran out of milk, so I took the empty milk container and I asked the soldiers if I could go and purchase some milk for the children. They started shouting at me saying, "No!" I begged them until they agreed, so I walked to Abu Haza's shop. Luckily, I found that he had some milk left.

I felt I wanted to know what was happening in the Sahah, so I went to higher ground to see. I saw that everything was destroyed, all of the homes were leveled to the ground. There were tanks and many soldiers. There was a group of soldiers, and a young man walking in front of them. He was raising his hands in the air. I looked closer and realized that it was Abu Jandal. I stayed to see what they were going to do to him. They had him stand up and they started hitting him with the butts of their guns. They tied his hands in front of him, and they started shouting savagely, although I did not understand what they were saying. They had him sit on the rubble of the Hadi family's house. They shot him in the face and in the head. I went back running to the house sobbing, I realized that there were more people in the house, all handcuffed. I looked at them and I cried, "They executed Abu Jandal." Some people cried, "We don't believe you!" I said, "It's the truth."

Three days later, I took my daughter and another neighbor lady and went to check on Abu Jandal. We saw him still sitting the same way he was when they executed him, sitting on his knees. I thought that maybe he was wounded and we could save him. His face was covered with blood—he was dead. It wasn't until a few days later that the soldiers allowed medical workers to collect bodies from the streets and homes. Some of these bodies were brutally maimed. Some of the medical workers asked me to help them collect the bodies and tell them the whereabouts of Abu Jandal's body.

You know, I have been in the camp for twenty-two years, and I have helped raise some of these young men. They started showing me bodies to identify Abu Jandal. I told them, "Abu Jandal was wearing khaki pants and a jacket." They unzipped a bag and I looked in to behold the body of Abu Jandal. I said, "This is him." It seems that the soldiers came back and burned his face. May God bless him and comfort his soul and all those young men who died for us. We have lost everything. But we have no regrets, we were and are still very proud. We will continue to resist.

Um Ali's oldest son is in an Israeli prison. He lost an eye as a result of the Israeli shelling.

Um Jamal

Um Jamal, is what the friends of Fathi Muhammad Suliman al-Shalabi call her. She is 68 years old, has white hair and wears a simple dress. To support her family she had a small grocery shop. But the shop was destroyed along with her house during the invasion. We tried to comfort her as much as we could as she sobbed throughout the entire interview.

On the day of the invasion, my children were all in the house. My husband was there too, and my brother-in-law, his wife, and children were also there. So were the neighbor's children, who are mostly girls. Once our home came under fire, we moved to my brother-in-law's house. Just one hour after we arrived, that house came under attack too. We did not know that the Israeli army was all over the neighborhood. One of the shells that fell on my brother-in-law's house wounded his wife in the chest. Some of the mattresses caught on fire and we rushed to put out the fires. We contemplated leaving but couldn't because they were shelling the house from several directions. My husband and I carried Jamal my son who is paralyzed, because a wheelchair is useless in rubble. We moved him to his uncle's house.

Now, the army was taking over all the homes making it nearly impossible to move around. Jamal had no idea what was happening around him. If you feed him, he will eat. If you don't, he doesn't. He is helpless like a little child. He is thirty-eight years old now. Since the first day, I have taken care of him, from feeding him to putting him to sleep.

We had to move to another home, and we had to leave Jamal at his uncle's home. Then tanks came and started toppling the wall of the house that we were in. My husband and other men broke the window and lowered a ladder to the street so we could escape. My sister-in-law who was wounded also came with us. Blood was still rushing out of her chest.

We found a tank in the street where we were fleeing. A soldier stepped out and ordered, "Men go this way and women that way." They had us stand several meters apart. My brother-in-law's son Abdullah was ordered to expose his stomach. They ordered him to turn around and they prepared to shoot him. We started screaming, "For God's sake, don't shoot him!" Finally, they had him stand facing the wall. They called on us one by one. They took all the men and ordered all the women to move back to my brother-in-law's house. But on our way back another army unit blocked our way and they shouted, "Go back!" I said, "Didn't you just tell us to return to our home and now you are telling us to go back, what should we do, fly in the air?"

We had to disperse. My sister-in-law went to the house of Hassan al-Tahbash. And others went to other places. My daughter and I tried to go to the Tahbash house, but the soldiers wouldn't let us, so I took my daughter and we ran back to my brother-in-law's house. We tried to take my son Jamal but twice the soldiers stopped us. I was so afraid for the safety of my son. After getting him out of the house, two children from the neighbor's house came and said, "Auntie, let us help you with your son, Jamal." The soldiers shouted at them to stay away. Then the soldiers took me after they ordered me to leave my son. What could I do? It was out of my hands. If it was up to me I would have carried him with my teeth, but they wouldn't let me. I told the soldiers, "My son is paralyzed." They said, "Take him back inside the house." So I did. We went back inside my brother-in-law's house.

The shelling was continuing and the second floor of the house we were in caught on fire after a shell landed inside. At this time I was with my son and daughter. I fed my son and gave him a drink of water. I changed his diaper. The next day I took a white scarf and we went outside. I could not carry Jamal alone, so I left to find help. Every time a tank saw us, I would wave the white scarf so they wouldn't hurt us. We managed to enter into a neighbor's house, they were so surprised that we'd managed to get in. I said, "God was looking after us." Many people from the neighborhood were on the first floor of that house. The second floor was full of soldiers. I had my son's ID with me. That's all that I managed to rescue.

I went up the stairs and one of the soldiers saw me. "I beg you," I said, "my son is over there by himself. He is paralyzed, he can't eat or drink on his own." Three older women from our neighborhood came to help me convince the soldiers to let me bring my son.

"The commander is taking a nap," said the soldier.

"Taking a nap or not taking a nap," I said, "I need my son!"

Oh, how much I cried that day, but finally a soldier said, "Okay, go get him."

"I am an old woman, I cannot do it on my own," I explained, "I need someone strong to come with me."

"You can take some girls with you," he said. I took a girl from the neighbor's, my daughter Basmah, and we went to bring him out.

At that time, a bulldozer was demolishing the neighbors' homes. We arrived to the house and we found that the cupboard had fallen. Part of the wall had fallen on my son. He was alive but he was screaming in pain. My son has never spoken a word in his life. My daughter looked at him and said, "Brother, we will try to move the debris." For the first time in his life he spoke, and he cried out, "Oh Allah, Oh Allah!"

The bulldozer started pushing the house down while we were inside. "Stop! Stop!" we screamed. But the driver wouldn't listen. We finally had to run out, leaving Jamal under the rubble. I was screaming, "My son, my son is inside!" The Israeli soldiers shouted back at me and the women—they called us whores.

Jamal will never disappear from my mind. For three days he remained alive under the rubble. He was buried with the house.

Jamal's body was never recovered from under the rubble. Um Jamal was devastated by the loss of her son Jamal—only forty days after the death of another son, Muhammad. Muhammad worked as a guard for the Palestinian Authority. He was killed by the Israelis on February 28, 2002, his birthday. Um Jamal went to the hospital to check on him under the impression that he had a minor leg injury. She found him in the hospital's morgue. It was very difficult for her to focus on one story at a time, as the tragedies in her life are many.

Adnan al-Ghul

Adnan al-Ghul is 45 years old, dark-skinned, tall and of medium build. He is gentle spirited. His hands were folded during the entire interview. He is very shy and polite. He is the father of three children, Ali (6), Mae (3), and Muhammad (2).

I live in a house located near the UN school. When the Israelis entered the camp, they entered from the western side during the night. There were a very large number of tanks and ground-troops. The army met fierce resistance in that part of the camp. Of course, the warplanes never stopped bombing the camp throughout the whole ordeal. Water, electricity, and phone lines were all cut off. My children were terrified—they lived through real horror. They would look from the window and say, "Daddy, the tanks are coming," or, "Daddy, the soldiers are over here!" The children were so scared, they would urinate on themselves. Even my two year old boy, Muhammad, his first word was "tanks"—and things like this.

My wife, who is a very strong woman, was so scared for the safety of our children, especially as missiles began landing on our neighbors' homes. We had some food saved in the house. I was also very worried for the safety of my family and friends who lived in the camp.

The number of Israeli soldiers and tanks was so massive, I never imagined something like this could ever happen. I saw the Israelis carrying many bodies outside the camp. I wasn't able to see faces, but there were many of them. My brother was one of those in the camp who was beaten and abused and arrested by the Israelis. He worked for the United Nations, he showed them his card, but they didn't care. They ridiculed him, they said, "Are you Kofi Annan?" They had him tied, handcuffed and left him in an abandoned house for three days, naked. Then they took him to Salem, where he endured days of abuse before they released him.

My cousin was wounded, another cousin was in the resistance, and is now in prison. Just a week ago, another cousin was killed. The Israelis threw his body near an open field close to the camp. One of my relatives, Rizek, was shot. They threw him beside Harsch Al-Saada, a large orchard near the camp. He crawled on his hands and knees all the way back to the camp. I still wonder if it is all true.

153

Khaoulah Damaj

Khaoulah Khaled Muhammad Damazj lives in a very well-kept, two-story house. She is 30 years old, dark, and short. She works in Al-Ansar Kindergarten. She comes from a large family.

My brother was wounded during the invasion. He was detained immediately. When the army entered the Damaj neighborhood, the resistance stood up to them. Our neighbor's son, Nasser Ghareeb was martyred. The Israelis then brought bulldozers and started toppling the houses. The *shebab* retreated to the Hawashin neighborhood. The army took over the mosque and the kindergarten. They entered the mosque, destroyed the doors, and vandalized everything. They also wrecked everything in the kindergarten.

Those who have done this to our mosque and kindergarten are criminals. I cannot describe with mere words what they have done. They even stole the money that the kindergarten collects to buy candy for the children. They broke every toy. They even took and destroyed the things in the snack shop. When the children ran to check on their kindergarten after the invasion, they stood and looked and said nothing. They were so shocked to see what was done to their toys and to their classrooms.

The mosque in the Damaj neighborhood experienced incomprehensible destruction. Israeli soldiers spread their own excrement throughout the mosque. They destroyed all the electronic equipment, the speakers, and the microphones. They urinated in bottles and placed them everywhere. They stole the money that people donated in the donation box. The Qurans were torn and thrown on the floor, with boot marks on them. All the curtains were torn, some thrown to the street. Nearly two hundred soldiers were in the mosque when the resistance retreated to the Hawashin neighborhood. They made the mosque their center. Now the mosque is closed and uninhabitable, as is the kindergarten.

Kauthar Zbyde

Kauthar Zbyde (20) is sweet, strong-willed, and she speaks with courage. Her home is very plain and humble. Her family lives in dire poverty.

When the Israelis invaded, we were in our house. We immediately sought shelter in my father-in-law's house, since it was safer. But soon after, my in-law's house came under fire. Resistance here was fierce, even though the *shebab* were fighting with simple weapons. We moved to a third house, but this time there was no escape. The house was attacked and we couldn't run out. We were nearly thirty people in the house, old and young. We all ran and took shelter in the bathroom. The *shebab* outside had plenty of faith but they had little food and water. So we used to risk our lives to sneak some food out for them. They would say, "Don't do that again, you don't want to get killed."

When we were trapped in the bathroom, once the shelling would cease for a moment, we used to try to listen to see if the *shebab* were still there. We used to feel a great sense of relief once we heard them talking outside.

My brother Taha was with the resistance. Those who were with him said Taha was the head of the resistance in his group. He used to be so worried about the safety of the people. My sister's fiancé went to that area once during the invasion. Taha told him to go back, saying, "Are you going to make my sister a widow before you are even married?"

Taha was killed by a sniper. After he was killed, they fired shells at him and completely burned his body. This was in the Damaj neighborhood. The *shebab* gathered what remained of him and put him in a house. Since that day, that house has been known as "The house of the hero." Then we brought him, and buried him near our house temporarily before we took him to the Martyrs' graveyard. For some reason I did not expect that Taha would be killed.

My mother was a resistance fighter too. She was fifty-one years old when she was martyred. She spent her life going from one prison to another. My father, God bless his soul, was also a resistance fighter, as were all my brothers. My mother was a woman who was loved by everyone. Yes, she was fifty-one, but we felt like she was from our generation. She treated us with respect and understood each one of us

Kauthar Z'byde

separately. She was very much respected by all of the fighters. When she was martyred, we were outside of our house. We were told that the Israelis would destroy our house at any moment. She was with us when we moved to our in-law's house. She was very nervous about the safety of her sons. She kept moving from one window to the other. Just before we realized the danger, snipers opened fire. She was hit with two bullets in the heart. Once she turned around, she was hit in the back. We did not realize that she was wounded because she ran for a distance.

Once she fell on the ground, we assumed that she just fainted from shock. But then blood poured out of her nose and mouth. I didn't know what to do but scream. I had a strange feeling, my mother was looking at me, and I was trying to understand what could she possibly want to say in her last moment of life. Our neighbor lady looked at her and said, "Just proclaim, 'There is no God but Allah'." Then she died.

Once the resistance fighters knew that she had been killed, they came to the house in four cars. Taha refused to come, he was in the Damaj neighborhood. He said, "I will not come to see my mother until I avenge her." He was able to strike a tank, then he came to say good bye. My relationship with my brothers is very strong because of my mom. We are all strong friends. I still see my brother Taha in my dreams. In my dreams, he opens the door and then he comes and starts joking with me. Then he goes and I start crying, asking him to come back.

In Jenin, the Zbyde home is considered a house of resistance. Taha was killed during the invasion. He was to be married a week after he was shot dead by a sniper. He was a leader in Al-Quds Brigade, the military wing of the Islamic Jihad movement. His brother Yahya was arrested during the invasion. Zakaria is on Israel's list of most wanted Palestinian fighters. Their mother Samira was killed in an earlier Israeli invasion of the camp.

Rund al-Shalabi

Rund Mustafa Abdelrahim al-Shalabi is in the fifth grade and attends an elementary school in Jenin that is funded and operated by the United Nations. She is the top student in her class. She is a beautiful, eleven-year-old girl with very strong character. Her eyes are full of determination and sadness. She speaks freely and with wisdom beyond her years.

I had a great father. No other father was like him. He was a member of the resistance. He defended his land and his children. My father was a very good man. He always murmured Quran and religious sayings. The last time he came to the house, he came to take some clothes to the resistance fighters. That was during the last invasion. He left and came back again to get a lantern. He often came back to the house during the battle to wash and pray. The last time he came, he stayed for a long time. He had us all sit down around him, and he ate with us. On that same day he was killed. He was killed on a Friday, a day that is blessed for Muslims.

On that day, my mother asked my cousin to go the area where my father was fighting. My mom and my brothers were terrified by the army. If anything fell, they would say, "The army is coming!" They were afraid of everything. Our life was consumed by fear. My mother asked my father if she should take us and flee the house. She said we had been suffering for days, were running out of food, and all my brothers and sisters were terrified. My father told her to stay home. They had a long discussion afterwards. I was also very terrified.

In those days, my mother was constantly reading Quran and praying. One of my brothers didn't know how to read, so my mother would teach him how to recite prayers that would help protect us from the army. We stayed this way until the eleventh day. It was then that the Israeli army moved into our house. They broke the door and stormed in shouting dirty words. We had been sleeping, but we immediately jumped out of our beds. My brothers were not very scared, but my mom and I were terrified. I was shivering from fear.

The soldiers filled the courtyard, they had all kinds of equipment with them. They shot and killed our sheep. They had a man from the neighborhood who knew some Hebrew translate. Then they used us as shields. They broke our cupboards, our beds, and a coat tree. I was scared but I didn't cry.

After the invasion, I went to Switzerland to talk about our suffering during the invasion. I brought all kinds of toys for my brothers when I came home, because here you don't have the chance to get toys. Here, if you go to the market, the tanks come and start shooting. I brought a toy tank for my brother. But when the army returned to our house after I had returned home, they broke all the toys.

The Israeli soldiers made my mom sit on her knees, and they pointed a gun to her head, and asked, "Where are the *shebab*?" They had a female soldier search my mother. She also beat my mom up and took her money.

"God is stronger than you," my mom told them.

The soldiers laughed and asked, "Where is your husband?"

"My husband is dead," she replied.

"No, my father is a martyr!" shouted my brother.

"Your father is a son of a bitch!" shouted the soldiers.

Once they knew that my father was a martyr, they kept coming back to our house, they used the area in front of our house as a base for their tanks. One of the soldiers took his clothes off and started dancing as another took our drum and started playing music. We sat in the corner, they wouldn't let us move for five hours. They wouldn't allow us to drink either.

They came and they asked my mother, "Where are the weapons?"

"We have no weapons," she said. "You should be ashamed of yourselves! You call us terrorists, and you and your Sharon are the real terrorists. You come to our refugee camp, and you destroy it. What crime did our sheep commit to be killed?"

"Shut up!" shouted the soldiers back.

Two soldiers grabbed some sticks and pretended that they were having a sword fight. The soldiers said, "Look at us, we are better than the Arabs at this!"

"You are cowards!" said my brother in a loud voice.

The soldier laughed and hit my brother very hard in the face. My brother did not cry. But when they left, my mother scolded my brother.

"Are you crazy?" she asked. "What kind of nonsense is this? Do you want them to topple the house on us?" My brother said, "But they didn't have bulldozers."

As we cleaned the house another army unit came. My mother said, "Could you please leave us alone?"

"Shut up!" shouted the soldiers. "We are not done with you yet!"

They destroyed whatever they hadn't broken already. They stayed until sunset. My mother kept telling them, "What are me and my children doing to you? Don't you have hearts?

Rund Mustafa Abdelrahim al-Shalabi

You are terrifying my children." My mother finally started to weep. "Do whatever you want,"she said. "Kill us all if you want, if we die, we will go to Paradise. But what will happen to you when you die?"

"This is the last time I am going to tell you to shut up!" screamed a soldier after running up and putting a gun to my mother's head. They stayed for a few more hours. They would go to the kitchen and would use our pots and pans as a toilet, they cut up all of our mattresses with knives. They tore up our schoolbooks and they burned our school bags. They got very mad when the saw a picture of a Palestinian flag in one of the books.

Before, I used to play all kinds of games. I used to play on the swing set and on the slide. Me and my best friend used to spend our days playing, and my brothers used to play soccer. But now we only play "Arabs and Israelis." It is also difficult to find kids who want to be Israelis, even though the Israelis always get to destroy the Arabs' houses.

When I grow up, I want to be a doctor, to treat the wounded with the will of God. My brother wants to be a teacher, and my other brother also wants to be a doctor. My father was poor, but he would take us to the market and say, "Choose whatever you want." During the invasion, he told us that he was going to build us a swing set and a garden and a special room to do our homework. He used to say, "You will get the chance to play with all the children in the neighborhood." But unfortunately God has chosen him to be a martyr. We are now on our summer vacation, although all of our schools were destroyed by the army.

Rund constantly speaks about her father and how much she loved him. Her grades remained high even after his death, because she said he wanted her to be a good student.

Mustafa & Muhammad Faed

Mustafa is the son of Hosni Faed and Muhammad, his cousin is the nephew of Hosni Faed. Mustafa is shy and quiet. Muhammad is very bold and interrupted Mustafa several times during the interview. Although the boys are cousins, they look and act more like brothers. They are both pre-teen boys.

Mustafa: The Israelis came down from the mountain and the clashes began. We gathered in one room in the house. The resistance fighters were in the street. For a whole week the shooting did not stop. My sisters were crying. My father was there, and he was making fun of things. It was his way of trying to make us feel better. When the airplane started bombing my mom would say, "Lay on the ground!" My father would say, "Don't listen to her!" and he would laugh. My father's name was Hosni.

When the resistance was gone, the Israelis managed to enter the camp. The Israelis took over the mosque and started shelling the houses. We hid in the basement. But the Israelis came and entered our house. They destroyed all of our food and they stepped on our bread. They destroyed the mirrors and the cupboards. The next day around six in the morning, they started calling on the men to assemble. We thought that the soldiers were far away but they were very close because they started shooting at the house. They shouted, "Open the door!" My mother opened the door and told them that my father was half deaf. They entered and started destroying everything again. They took my father and started beating him up—really bad. We heard him screaming with pain. When they finished beating him, they took him with them. We looked for him for three months. The Israelis wouldn't admit that they had him.

Three months later, they told us that he was dead and they had his body in Abu Kibir, a morgue in Jerusalem. When they arrested him, he survived for a while, but they tortured him a lot, and he fainted several times. The Israelis wouldn't treat him. My uncle Ahmed was with him and he told us this.

Muhammad: My father was with my uncle Hosni when he was martyred. My uncle was taken as a human shield to knock on doors for the soldiers. They had my father walking in front of them too. Then they had them sit in the street for a while. The soldiers came and pointed to some drawings on the wall where they were sitting and said, "What is this?"

"Nothing," said my uncle Hosni, "they are just kids' drawings."

"No," barked the soldier, "these are maps for the *shebab*."

The soldiers started to beat him up. Then they took them both on a tank and threw them in Harsh Al-Saada. (Harsh Al-Saada is an area neighboring the camp, used as a point of assembly for Israeli forces. Residents of the camp were also gathered there and tortured before being transferred to other detention centers.) They were left in this area for three hours, and then they were taken to Salem. My uncle Hosni fainted and started making sounds, people thought he was dying. My father started shouting, "This man is dying, this man is dying!" Then my Israelis took my uncle Hosni, and we didn't know what happened to him. We kept calling hospitals and everyone would say, "We don't have this name." Finally, the Palestinian Authority contacted the Israelis who said that he was dead. The Israelis had, for a while, claimed that it was the resistance who killed him. We know that they are lying.

When I grow up, I want to be a resistance fighter.

Hosni Faed was a very simple man. He was a good friend to many people in the camp. He was beaten with the handle of a shovel by the Israelis. The Israelis finally admitted that Hosni Faed died in an Israeli prison. Witnesses confirmed that he was beaten again after he was arrested.

Jamal al-Shalabi

Jamal Munther al-Shalabi is 12 years old and in the seventh grade. He is very thin and is darkened by the sun. His eyes are small and brown. He doesn't hesitate to speak. His wish is to be a doctor when he grows up. He lives in a very simple house that was severely damaged by the Israelis.

The first day we heard that the Israelis were trying to invade the camp we were not very concerned. They had attacked our camp many times in the past. The airplanes began bombing and tanks were firing at the camp. Young men went to the street and took whatever weapons were available to defend us. My family ran and gathered in one room in the house, and I couldn't go to the bathroom. We could hardly breathe in that small room. My father said that a missile fell just beside us, on our grandfather's house. My father ran outside barefoot, and had to run over the shattered glass. He couldn't open the door to my grandfather's home. He jumped through the window, and he rescued my grandfather.

In the next few days, the Israelis started telling us to leave our homes, so we went to the Sahah. Blood was everywhere. There was a body lying in the street covered with maggots. We saw the bulldozers destroying houses, and tanks were everywhere. My father and our neighbor's son were with us. The Israelis ordered them to approach. The Israelis made them stand beside a wall and ordered the rest of us to leave. We kept on walking until we saw a tank blocking the street. We thought maybe we should run away and hide in one of the houses. But the soldiers crouched upon their knees as if they wanted to shoot at us. So we thought we better continue walking toward them. It was scariest when they started calling to my brother on the loudspeaker, "You with the blue shirt, come over here!"

Finally, they had us leave the camp. A tank followed very close behind us. I felt as if it was going to run us over. A bulldozer passed by us as we were walking. The driver of the bulldozer looked at us and started yelling nasty words at us.

When I grow up, I want to be a doctor. My friend, Muhammad Umar Hawashin was martyred when he was in the sixth grade. He was hit with two bullets, one in his chest and one in his stomach. He was the best friend I ever had. May God drive the occupation soldiers away from our homes. They are so unfair. What kind of business do they have coming to our homes and treating us this way? This is mean.

Um Muhammad

Um Muhammad, whose given name is Naemi Abu Atea, is 54 and has nine daughters and six sons. Despite the dramatic events she experienced during the attack, she says that her faith in God has grown stronger and gives her hope.

On the sixth day of the invasion, part of our neighbor's house collapsed. Our family was hiding in our basement. We were about twenty-five people. The children were screaming and missiles were falling. As every missile or shell that fell, everything would shake and the children would start crying. It was then I would say, "Just pray and things will be all right."

One day, the Israelis broke into the house. I said, "What do you think you are doing? You are terrifying the children!" The soldiers said, "Leave your house right now." I said, "I have nowhere to go." They forced us into groups of men and women separately. Then they took the men and left. Some soldiers stayed in our house for nearly five days. We did not know that some of our men were taken to Salem. The soldiers went to the upper floor. They collected everything that breaks and threw it from the top of the house. It was entertainment for them.

We had our life savings in a small bag hidden in our bedroom. The soldiers found it when they were searching the house. They took the money, and my girls started crying. I said, "We have faith in God, and he is there to take care of us."

On the eleventh day, the soldiers ordered us to leave the house. Some soldiers dragged an eighty-two-year-old woman towards us from the camp. They said, "Take her with you." We carried her as we walked in the night. We sought shelter in another house in the neighborhood. The neighborhood, however, had no water, no electricity—nothing.

Over there, five people died when a missile hit the roof of their house, and here three others were killed—all in the same day.

Um Muhammad pointed first to a destroyed house in one direction and then to another damaged house in the opposite direction.

I knew some of the people who died, but not all of them. They were killed and left for twelve days without burial. It was very difficult to

169

Um Muhammad

tolerate the smell. But the Israelis wouldn't let anyone take the bodies out. We left the camp but returned when the invasion was over. I came back to my house and found the upper floor completely burned. The streets were filled with rubble and shattered glass. Nothing in our house was left unbroken, no matter how big or small.

This was a criminal act. How can anyone in this world be so brutal? We merely ask God that these days are never repeated again. I pray for peace for the whole world. Just recalling the way that the children were screaming is very difficult for me. Our children grow up so fast. Now the children whose fathers were killed keep talking about wanting to avenge their fathers. I don't know if words have any value anymore. If we talk forever, will this rid us from the occupation?

Adilah Ahmed Turkman

Adilah, 42, is a simple woman with a round face and a scarf that is carefully wrapped around her hair and face. She continued wearing the scarf very carefully, even as she lay wounded in a hospital bed. When she revealed the part of her face and neck under the scarf, there were large caverns from a bullet that carved a painful, deep line from behind her ear, down her neck, to her upper back.

I was home when the Israeli army entered the area around two in the afternoon, on September 11, 2001. There were some resistance fighters who came to our side of the camp and asked for water to drink. I went out accompanied by a relative, to give them some water. There was an Israeli plane in the air, although the camp was quiet. Once I gave them water, I heard bullets. I told the young men to run. Just as I finished my words, I felt that my right arm become heavy. I lost any feelings in it. I was baffled. I looked around when another bullet hit my face. Then I fainted. The neighbors took me to the Jenin hospital. I was in critical condition. A resistance fighter who was also a member in the Palestinian Authority Security Forces and had asked for the water was also wounded. He was hit in the arm. He managed to drink before we both were shot. The bullets fell all around us like rain.

The Israelis tried to enter the camp to the Sahah. They couldn't get all the way in, because the resistance fighters blocked their entry. That day thirteen martyrs fell in the camp. One of them was my cousin, Eyad Masri. Eyad was nineteen years old. He was shot earlier in the afternoon. He passed by my doorstep half an hour before he was shot. I told him to be careful. We spoke briefly.

Later, three tank shells fell on the school where he was. We knew that some people were hurt. I finished praying and went outside. A few young men were running with a helmet and what appeared to be the remains of a person. I didn't realize that it was the head of my cousin Eyad until they drew near. He was hit directly by a shell. Shelling took place from a distance as my cousin and his colleagues stood near the school.

Adilah remained in critical condition in the Jenin hospital for three days, then was transferred to Al-Razi hospital. Weeks later she recovered but her wounds were fresh and her pain intolerable. For the sake of her family, she decided to return to the camp. Only months later, the April invasion began.

Resistance is usually focused around the entrance of the camp. I lived in a house right by the entrance, also close to the courtyard. The first thing the Israeli soldiers do when they invade is station themselves in the Sahah. They take over the houses, mostly tall ones near the Sahah, and there they position their snipers.

I was in my home on the first day of the invasion. Since the first thing they do is to shell the Sahah, my family and I feared that the Israelis would kill us right away. So we moved to my in-laws' house, located in the Damaj neighborhood. It was safer there, we thought.

We wanted to all be together. We stayed there for four days. During these days, the Israeli soldiers were not able to enter the camp. They kept on attacking and shelling from the outside. On the fifth day, they resorted to aerial bombardment. They knew that the resistance was too strong, thus they used warplanes to destroy them. The planes fired missiles everywhere. I was sitting with my daughters talking in the middle of one room when a missile struck a house near us. There was a huge explosion and shrapnel flew all around our house. I gazed at my daughter as she fell on her back with a large wound in her chest. She was not able to feel her wound right away as she put her hands on her ears and screamed, "I cannot hear, I cannot see." Blood gushed out of her chest but thank God, no shrapnel got inside her chest. The windows shattered, the doors collapsed. A young man came crawling on his hands and knees into our house. He was bleeding. His name was Hilal Jalamneh. He was twenty-three years old. He was bleeding in the neck as shrapnel from the missile had struck him. We pulled him in and we did all that we could do to help. He left the home in very bad condition and I never saw him after that. However, now we learned that he was arrested soon after and remains in an Israeli jail.

Early the next day, we realized that a bulldozer had entered the camp. We heard it toppling our neighbors' homes. Only one bulldozer entered our block. We listened as it moved up the street, demolishing houses in its way. Finally, it stopped near my in-laws' house. We were all in one room. We wanted to be together as we always do in times like these. The upper floor began falling. It fell as we watched. We initially assumed that they were planning to topple the parts of the house that were blocking their tanks from going up the street. But we didn't realize that they were planning to dump the wreckage on us as we helplessly stood in the first floor. We began screaming as the bulldozer closed in on us. There were many of us: myself, my husband, two sons and four daughters, my mother-in-law and her daughter, and two of my brothers-in-law and their children. We held our scarfs up and waved them, begging the soldiers to stop. We screamed at them, "Fear God, what are you doing? We have children. Where are you going?" They said nothing. They kept on toppling the house. The resistance fighters heard us screaming and came to our rescue. They threw hand grenades at the bulldozer. The soldiers and the bulldozer began retreating. There was a small door in the back of the house. We escaped from that door, with the help of the fighters, all the way to another home nearby. We couldn't escape the camp. It was completely sealed. We were in a basement. This time, our numbers grew to over fifty people.

When we ran to the other house we saw the destruction inflicted on the camp. Many houses were leveled to the ground. It was devastating. We were all in one basement and we stayed there for six days. We had a small jar of olives and a medium size jar of water. Adults would not drink unless it was an absolute necessity and they would drink very little. We made the children drink with the cap of the jug. We also had a carton of eggs. We had many children who used to cry most of the time from hunger and thirst. We also couldn't go to the bathroom outside or let the children go, for the snipers were stationed on the Al-Ansar Mosque and could see us.

We couldn't talk to our neighbors or go outside, but we knew that there was still resistance in the camp. We could hear the young men passing back and forth near the house. We could also hear the army tanks roaring nearby, sometimes stopping by the house or moving up and down the streets. We couldn't sleep from fear, especially as missiles fell on our neighborhood day and night.

Abdelkarim Sadi was our neighbor. He worked for the camp's municipality collecting garbage. I know him as well as I know myself. He had nothing to do with the resistance. Israeli soldiers entered his house. They put him in one of the house's corners and ordered him to take all of his clothes off. Then they shot him—right before his family. They threw him in the street, close to his family's home. He stayed there for eleven days. No one dared to touch him because of the snipers. He decomposed because of the sun, and flies were feeding on his body. I saw him on the twelfth day.

On the ninth day of the invasion, however, many soldiers caught us hiding inside. They stormed the house, there were so many. The soldiers divided us in two groups. They took the young men and interrogated them separately. My sons were beaten badly. They were questioned about names of resistance fighters. "Where is Tawalbe?" they asked. Mahmoud Tawalbe was the head of the resistance in the camp. They punished them hard and slapped them—both of my sons, even my sixteen-year-old. The interrogation and beating lasted for five hours. We were screaming because we thought that the Israelis executed them. Later, they came out with bloody and bruised faces. Thank God for everything, good and bad.

On the twelfth day, the Israeli army called on loudspeakers for the people of the camp to leave, otherwise they threatened to bulldoze the homes on us. By that time, they had already demolished most the camp's neighborhoods anyway. The Hawashin, Abu Sibah, and the Damaj neighborhoods were already destroyed, but they wanted to humiliate the people further. We left, just my four daughters and I, and went to the town of Jenin for two days.

We passed by the soldiers on our way out. We were terrified. I saw two dead bodies of Palestinians in the street, but I couldn't recognize their faces. Four young men were handcuffed and tied to a pole near the mosque. They were stripped naked. We didn't realize that Israelis soldiers were inside the mosque. We felt that we must help the young men but they began gesturing with their hand for us to leave and to keep on walking. It was then that we understood why the young men didn't want us to help them. The soldiers were hiding in the mosque. So we kept on walking.

Four days later, we sneaked back in to our house near the entrance of the camp. I was extremely worried about my family and wanted to know if they managed to come back home. No one was there, and I couldn't open the door with my house key. But then we realized that we didn't need to open the door because the Israeli soldiers had opened large holes in most of the house walls to create shortcuts through the neighborhood. Half of our house was completely burned. All of our furniture was destroyed. Our new mattresses that we were saving for special occasions were ripped. The soldiers urinated on our clothes and stole most of the tools in my husband's carpentry shop. Even the furniture that my husband had finished for some customers was set on fire. We had nothing left. Everything was gone. Homes around mine were also destroyed—some were burned completely, others heavily damaged, and many demolished. I learned that another neighbor of ours, Rabee, was shot and killed by a sniper as he tried to save a wounded man. He died instantly.

The thing that broke my heart the most was an old man with asthma that we had staying with us at my in-laws'. He died as a result of tear gas that soldiers kept dumping inside people's homes. It was early in the morning when his daughter came running, saying that her father was sick and not responding to her. I was the first to arrive at his bedside. I felt his heart and he was dead. We carried him with us as we left the camp.

Almost everyone has stories to tell of homes bulldozed on top of entire families and of missing people—many of them. Most of the houses destroyed in the Hawashin neighborhood were destroyed by missiles—the people had no chance to run away.

When we came back, we only thought of checking on other people, our neighbors.

Adilah Ahmed Turkman

175

Adilah went to Amman two weeks after the invasion. The pain in her back increased, and surgery became a necessity. Her family is still in the camp. Her wounded daughter is doing better. Their house is severely damaged, but her family has no other place to go. Every time a missile lands near their home they say, "There is no God but Allah." They felt that death was coming with every missile. The children were reading Quran. Her youngest is Sanabel, who is eight years old. During the attack, Sanabel fainted several times. She kept asking questions, "When are we going to die? Are they going to kill us now?"

During this time, we did not expect any outside help. We only had faith in the resistance. We shared our food with the fighters. I used to send our children to bring some fighters to share the few bites we had.

It was horrible. It was beyond words. Chunks of flesh and bloodied kaffiahs were in the streets. We screamed when we saw them as we fled the camp. I saw bodies, body parts, the hair of a girl, legs, and fingers that were found under the rubble. Not many bodies were found in one piece. Seven bodies were recovered as I watched. When the Israeli soldiers stormed my in-laws' house, they told us, "Forget that you have a camp, forget something called Jenin. We will destroy it."

I will not leave Jenin. This is my home. I have nowhere else to go.

The resistance was so strong. I wish there were more like them. They stayed all the day singing and chanting. The wounded fighters filled us with spirit. I wanted to go out and sing with them. They fought until the end. They died heroes. They died martyrs.

Hussein Barakat

Adilah's husband Hussein Zidan Barakat is a short, fifty-year-old. His dark, wrinkly face told stories before he even spoke. He accompanied his wife Adilah at the hospital, busily serving her. He was hesitant to talk to us at first for fear that the Israelis would detain him on his way back to the West Bank. Finally he agreed to talk. He wears an old yet handsome blue suit with a tie. He clutches a cigarette releasing lots of smoke.

I am a carpenter. I have a carpentry shop in the camp located in the same house I live. We expected the invasion of the camp, but what we didn't expect was an invasion of such magnitude, with warplanes, missiles, and the rest. No one expected such brutality. Many residents, however, received the invasion with eagerness. They were ready to confront the soldiers who have for long oppressed the camp and committed so many crimes here. The young men were cheering and residents of the camp were supportive. Groups of fighters roamed the streets of the camp chanting, "Allah *Akbar!*" ("God is great!")

The resistance fighters were mostly young men trained for such an occasion. They were separate from the average camp residents, although they are camp residents. However, the Israelis seemed not to distinguish between the residents or the fighters. Israelis toppled the homes on the people inside—I am one of them. If it hadn't been for God's help, my whole family and I would've died.

On the first day, although resistance was limited because the Israelis were shelling from the outside, the Israelis didn't enter the camp. In fact, they wouldn't enter for four days. They just kept on bombing us. The resistance was limited because it is not the kind able to face a large army. The *shebab* were waiting for the soldiers to enter the camp. To weaken the resistance and the camp altogether, the Israelis randomly fired inside the camp. Of course, those who paid the price were the civilians in the camp.

We escaped our home near the entrance of the camp on the second day. We moved to my family's house on the other side of the camp, in the Damaj neighborhood. On our way, we noticed that the streets were empty except for the resistance fighters. They were not many nor were they in large groups as one would expect. Each group was two or three at the most, gathered around the corners and in the alleyways. They were full of spirit. The kids waved to them, and they waved back.

The army entered on the fifth day. They entered with their bulldozers, tanks, and jeeps. They seemed to be in a panic, gunning down civilians, demolishing homes, and shooting at anything that moved. It's true that the resistance in the camp was tough, but no matter how tough it was, it was still inadequate. Most of the shooting and bombing came from the Israelis. The resistance grew even fiercer because the Israelis were demolishing homes on top of families and bombing at random. The fighters hoped to push the Israeli army back and help save as many lives as possible. It was then, toward the seventh day, that the Israelis intensified their bombardment from the air.

On the ninth day, over loudspeakers the Israelis told us to leave. They said if we didn't leave they would topple the homes on those remaining inside, and that they were preparing to shell the camp with F-16s.

I was still in the camp when I learned that my house had been burnt and parts of it leveled by tanks. I am glad that we left that house at the entrance of the camp. Keeping my family there would have been a costly mistake.

During the first few days, the damage in the camp was not as visible. The visible damage occurred after the fifth day, when thirteen Israeli soldiers were killed. I think that the Israeli army itself mistakenly killed the soldiers. Israeli planes shelled a building with the soldiers inside, thinking that they were resistance fighters. Thirteen soldiers were killed. That angered them very much. They seemed to be out to get everyone, civilians, fighters, and even animals. There was a horse that fled a burning house and was shot with four bullets by the Israelis. He was lying dead in front of my house. I realized that when we came back to our house after the invasion was over. I saw the dead horse lying at the doorsteps of my house. It was sad and the smell was horrid.

We only realized the incredible scale of damage once we moved from the house where we sought refuge at the Damaj neighborhood to another. We say that almost the entire area was leveled to the ground. The alleyways that were approximately four meters wide became fifteen meters wide. Where there once stood homes and clearly defined streets, there was nothing but ruins.

I personally didn't see any dead bodies in the street as we fled. I was too scared for the safety of my family to even look around. Soldiers were everywhere. Members of my family saw some bodies. However, I witnessed several cases decomposed bodies being pulled from under the rubble on the day after the invasion stopped. I personally saw seven people pulled from under the wreckage of the Hawashin neighborhood. They were all women and children. They were not fighters. We knew them well.

Anyway, when we left the camp for the town of Jenin, we were terrified—not for our lives, but for the lives of our children. The Israelis were declaring in Hebrew and in Arabic on the loudspeakers. They said that if you want to be killed, stay in the camp. We left in one group composed of nearly forty-five men, women, children, and elders. There was a man with asthma, an old man. He couldn't stand the smoke of the burning buildings and the smoke generated by the tanks and tear gas. He collapsed and died. We carried him with us like a child. I prepared him for burial. May God bless his soul.

Even when we moved to the town of Jenin, we were still not safe. We moved deeper into the town, for tank shells were hitting too close.

It was a horrifying experience for my family. In addition to the constant fear of being killed, there was the experience of my daughter when she was wounded by shrapnel. We were in the house we had escaped to in the Damaj neighborhood, when flying shrapnel burst the door open. A missile had fallen near the house. It opened a large wound in a girl's chest. Her mother, sisters and brothers began screaming. We called the Red Cross, but they said they were unable to reach the camp since the Israelis were not letting medical workers into the camp. I told my family there was nothing we could do, but to comfort her and pray. She stayed this way for three days before we managed to leave the camp into the town of Jenin.

I have a little girl in the third grade. I feel that she has aged several years during these few days. Every time a missile was fired into the camp I used to utter: "There is no God but Allah, and Muhammad is the prophet of Allah." She used to ask me: "Daddy, why do you keep saying that?" I often answered her, "By saying so, God will protect us from the missile." She believed me, and every time we came under attack, she used to say, "There is no God but Allah. Thank Allah for everything."

We returned to the camp after the twelfth day. We found the camp in ruins. My home was destroyed. Any houses that were still standing had large holes in the walls, were filled with broken furniture, were burnt, and looked as if they could fall at any moment. They robbed my carpenter shop. One of our neighbors that watched them destroy my house from a crack in his house, told me that he watched the soldiers as they took everything that could be carried from my shop. It's hard to describe the damage inside the house. They seemed to spare nothing. Even the blankets and pillows were torn apart.

Although we watched medical workers and emergency aid workers pulling body parts from under the rubble, I can only say thank God for everything. We remain strong and our spirit is still high. We have high spirits because we were the real victors. The Israelis failed to achieve their goals. They were there to suppress the resistance, to arrest our fighters. But they couldn't.

One of those I saw being pulled out from under the rubble was a little girl. You could still see her polished nails. Her hands and fingers were bent in a painful way. Beside the bodies that were still somewhat intact from when they were pulled out from under the rubble, we saw lots of flesh, hair, feet and legs. People piled them up saying, "This pile belongs to this family, and this pile belongs to that family."

I have nowhere else to go but back to my camp, to my house. No matter what they did, I will go back. I will live in the ruins if I have to. The only thing they can do is shoot and kill me. I will only leave my house a martyr. We have no hope that any help will come from the outside, only from God. He is the only one who stands by oppressed people.

When I left with my wife to Jordan, my eight-year-old was so upset, even mad at us. She didn't want to say good bye, she ran to the street, at five in the morning. She didn't want us to leave. She is still living in the ruined home. Once I get back, I will try to put our life together, to fix my shop and try to rebuild my house.

Kamal Fahmaoui

An enthusiastic thirty-four-year-old man, Kamal Fahmaoui was a member of the Palestinian Authority Security Forces. He fought and was wounded in the early days of the invasion of Jenin. He speaks with pride. His round face and bulky body stood in contrast to the thin, wounded arm, he holds tight to his chest. He regrets not dying for his camp. He was the last wounded man to be evacuated from the camp before the Israelis took control of all the access roads that led to Jenin. He constantly smokes.

The Israeli army has many bad names for our camp, but we call it the camp of martyrs. Many invasion attempts took place in the past, but the camp had yet to fall. Adilah was wounded during the fourth invasion. Muhammad was wounded in the last failed invasion, early in March. With each invasion the Israelis resorted to a new strategy, but the resistance, backed by the people of the camp, was always strong and alert.

On the last failed invasion, the one in early March, the Israelis conducted a tight siege. They surrounded the camp from four directions: from the south, in the mountain area known as Jawabra, from the East and West, and also from the North where a flat land is located, known as Sahl Ibn Amr. In the Sahl Ibn Amr area, the Israelis have a military camp. They used to hold detainees there, to interrogate and torture them. Within three days of the invasion over two dozen were killed. Amjad Fakhouri, one of the greatest freedom fighters was killed. However, the Israelis once again failed to conquer the small camp. We inflicted heavy damage on them. They only admit the killing of three soldiers, although I can assure you there were more. They left, also determined to return.

When the Israeli army came back for the invasion in which the massacre took place, it attacked the camp from seven locations. They focused their assault in the early days on the town of Jenin. Similar to the invasion that preceded it, most of the wanted were from the camp, so little fighting took place.

The relationship between the camp and town is very strong. There is no difference between being a resident of the camp or a resident of the town. I lived on the border of the camp as a resident of the town. I had many friends in the camp, I spend most of my time there. And that is where I was wounded.

There were many different resistance factions in Jenin and the camp representing various political parties and resistance movements. However, when we fought, we fought like one body. It made no difference being Hamas, Fatah, Islamic Jihad or any other. We shared our last bullets and our last bites of bread. I must also mention that most of the resistance came from members of the security forces. Some of them were on Israel's wanted list, and others have a long experience in resistance and have spent years in Israeli jails. We don't call them jails, but "universities of the resistance."

You might not believe me when I tell you that we were happy when we learned that the Israelis were staging an attack on the camp. We felt that we were receiving an old friend, but a cruel old friend. We wanted revenge for what they have done to us in the past, not only in the Jenin refugee camp, but for brutally killing our people throughout the years. You see, we can never forget their massacres in Sabra and Shatila, Kufer Kassim, or any other. But instead of us going to fight them, they were coming to us. We were ready with our bullets and explosives. We felt that this was a decisive battle. A day before the Israeli invasion, the resistance offered to help the residents of the camp to leave. Few left. The rest said that they would rather stay in their homes, support the resistance as much as they could, and fight with them if necessary.

Kamal Fahmaoui

On the first three days, the attack was equally distributed on the camp and the town. The resistance, on the second and third day, left the town and headed to the camp. I was one of them. The reason for such tactical withdrawal has something to do with the nature of the town itself. Fighting in the town with its large streets and wide space between its buildings was difficult. It was easy for the occupation army to spot and kill people. We moved to the camp because it was easier to fight there. Some of the camp's alleys

182

were so narrow that you have to walk sideways to squeeze through.

I was wounded two days later. Before being injured, it had been days since I had any sleep. It was late at night, and I had just finished my prayer. I asked God for martyrdom while defending my country. Shortly after, we came under attack and began regrouping. I was in an exposed area and needed to find a location that was safer. I ran toward an alley. Suddenly a barrage of bullets chased me. Shots were coming from an Israeli sniper who was positioned in an area that faced the camp's courtyard. I managed to reach an alleyway when I realized I was hit in the arm. I threw myself in a secured spot. My friends tried to reach me but the snipers kept showering that open area with bullets. I bled for an hour and a half. An ambulance finally was able to make it into the camp and rescued me.

I learned from the doctors at the hospital that I was the last wounded that was able to make it out of the camp. Those who were wounded after me stayed. The ambulance that tried to rescue me came under heavy attack. Most of those who were wounded after me bled to death, some were left to bleed in the alleyways. The doctor at the hospital told me I was lucky for being the last wounded to make it out. I told him, in fact, I am the most *unlucky* one for not having the honor to stay and fight with my friends and for not being a martyr.

The first day I was in the Jenin hospital, the hospital itself came under attack. Snipers located near the hospital opened fire on people as they stood by the windows. They shelled the oxygen room and burned other areas within the hospital. They fired at ambulances that tried to move out to rescue more wounded. You see, even the hospitals—something that the whole world agrees must be protected areas in times of war—were targets for the Israeli army.

During my stay there, a father and his daughter managed to sneak to the hospital. They were both wounded and struggled to walk. Holding onto each other and using a back street before the snipers discovered it, they got to the hospital. Shortly after the wounded father and daughter arrived, a nine-year-old who came to visit his father in the hospital used the same route and was spotted by an Israeli army sniper. He was shot dead. I saw a photo that the doctors took of him immediately after he was declared dead in the hospital. His head was split open, and the upper part of the head was completely gone. A Palestinian policeman, Munzer Al-Haj was wounded nearly ten meters away from the hospital's main gate. He was wounded in the leg and was bleeding heavily. The nurses tried to rescue him, but every time the nurses walked toward him, soldiers shot at them. Finally after bleeding and screaming for six hours, the young man died. The Israeli soldiers gave the nurses permission to bring his body inside.

In the hospital the situation was dire. They quickly ran out of food. I felt guilty asking for water. I drank once a day. We had little food and quickly ran out. When the Israelis knew that no more wounded were being brought in, they rounded up most of the nurses and the doctors and ordered them to go home. The doctors took me with them in one of the ambulances to another hospital, Al-Shifa—it was more secure and located deeper in the town.

I was still in touch with the fighters inside the camp, using a mobile phone. A hero we know as Abu Jandal, his real name was Yusuf Ahmed Kabha was then the leader of the resistance. He is a member of Fatah, and also a member of the Palestinian National Forces as well. He came to the camp a day before the invasion with a group of fighters. He was elected by the resistance to lead them into their expected fight with the occupation army. Originally, he is from a village called Yabad. He was with the Palestinian revolutionaries in exile and returned, along with many others, after the signing of the Oslo agreement. I know him very well. He was my teacher. He gave me a military training course in Jericho when I first joined the force.

He is very short, dark, and bald from the front. A disease left part of his mouth paralyzed on one side. Although he spoke with difficulty, he was a well-spoken and educated man. He was in his late thirties and married with eight children. In addition to Abu Jandal, there was Ziad al-Amr, the head of the Al-Aqsa Brigade. He killed three occupation soldiers in the first day of the invasion and took their automatic rifles. He was killed soon after.

Other heroes were Mahmoud Tawalbe, from the Saraya Al-Quds of the Islamic Jihad, and Mahmoud Abu Hilweh, the head of the Al-Qassam Brigade. They inflicted heavy losses on the enemy during the invasion. They were all martyred. They are all heroes. We are very proud of them. The Israelis needed a massacre, however, to kill these heroes. The Israelis walked across piles of civilian bodies to get to the resistance.

On the ninth day of the resistance, the Israelis declared that they would enter the camp at any price. The monster Sharon wanted to destroy the camp. But in actuality, it was an American massacre because it was conducted with American weapons, Apaches helicopters, bullets, and automatic rifles. Even their soldiers were trained and armed by the Americans. I have to also say that Arab regimes took part in the massacre by standing aside and watching as the camp was bulldozed and people died under the rubble.

It will be very difficult to go back to the camp. Many of the faces I once knew, men, women and children, all gone. Some are still under the rubble. Even Yusrah Abu Khorj is dead—she was retarded, for God's sake. They struck her with a shell as she stood in front of her house, blowing her to pieces. I saw her hair, the only thing that was left of her. There were people who were killed on the balconies of their homes, and many of them were civilians. Many of civilians joined the resistance during the invasion. They were not trained soldiers, or "terrorists" as Israel calls them. Mahmoud—the young man in the other room—he is not a soldier. He just joined the resistance because he couldn't stand doing nothing. Those who couldn't fight contributed some of the bread they had and some of the little water they had left. All of Jenin was part of the resistance, they are all heroes.

I returned to the camp following the invasion before I headed to Amman. It was devastating. It was inhumane. Hundreds of families were left homeless after their homes were shelled, burned, or bulldozed.

Despite everything, the resistance is not finished. Abu Jihad was killed, and Yahya Iyash came. Yahya was killed, Tawalbe came. Now Tawalbe was killed, and someone else will take his place. As long as there are Palestinian mothers who give birth, more heroes will be born. The resistance will never die.

Abdelrazik al-Hayjah

Abdelrazik Abu al-Hayjah, 55, is the Administrator of the Jenin refugee camp and oversees all the administrative affairs of United Nations Relief and Works Agency (UNRWA) in the camp. He has a large family, five sons and three daughters. He is neither tall nor short. He has dark skin and snow white hair. He is polite, very shy, and looks to the ground when he talks.

The invasion began on April 2, around seven-thirty in the evening. News stations began talking about Israeli army buildup coming from Salem and A'Rabeh, near Jenin. I started receiving telephone calls that scores of tanks and military vehicles were preparing to execute a large operation in Jenin. On April 3rd, around two-thirty in the morning, the Israeli forces approached the camp from three directions, west, north and south. "Special forces" began sneaking into nearby houses in those areas. Once they overwhelmed the areas close to them with shells and heavy artillery rounds, they started penetrating more areas. The media at that point greatly exaggerated, saying that there was a huge number of suicide bombers, fighters, land mines, and all sorts of nonsense. It seems to me that the Israeli soldiers themselves believed these exaggerations when they attacked the camp. They shelled homes with all kinds of weapons.

The Israeli forces began breaking into smaller units, each unit containing twenty to thirty soldiers. They would take over houses, set them up as outposts, and used the residents as human shields. They did this in all three directions, except to the east. It was left open for three days. The resistance was fierce in a way that exhausted the Israelis and scared them. The Israeli army was not able to enter the center of the camp until they completely bulldozed the Hawashin and the Damaj neighborhoods. The Israeli army tactic continued this way until the sixth and seventh day. It was then that Israeli warplanes participated heavily in the attack. Apaches and Cobras hovered over the camp, without a moment of rest, heavily shelling the camp. The *shebab* focused their resistance in the Hawashin neighborhood. They fought so hard that the Israeli army was getting desperate. Even the Hebrew newspapers said that the fighters enjoyed high spirits and legendary unity. They defended their dignity and their rights, and had untold faith in their cause, despite their rudimentary weapons and the fact that they were completely besieged.

After intense bombardment on the sixth and seventh day, the resistance quieted down. The Israelis were closing off the eastern side of the camp. The Israeli army moved to the Hawashin neighborhood. They were careless when they moved because they thought that they had destroyed the entire resistance. However, the *shebab* were about to ambush them. Unlike what the Hebrew media said, there wasn't a booby-trapped house, but fighters waiting for the soldiers until they drew near. There were many casualties among the Israeli soldiers. Thirteen soldiers were killed on the spot and others were wounded. Those who survived ran to nearby houses for shelter. They started screaming for help. They asked the *shebab* for a cease fire. The answer then was, "President Yasser Arafat was besieged by Israeli tanks in Ramallah, how do you expect the Palestinians to help you after all you have done?" There was turmoil among the Israelis. The Defense Minister and even Sharon himself came to the camp to investigate. It was then that they decided to bulldoze the entire area. They dispatched giant bulldozers and then they began systematic destruction, starting from the Damaj neighborhood, going all the way to, and including, the Hawashin neighborhood. They also toppled most homes in Sahah. We received some numbers regarding the damage resulting from the Israeli army's action. There were 176 buildings that were leveled to the ground, 320 buildings were severely damaged, 57 buildings were burned down and 2,000 buildings were partially damaged. I should also mention that the Israeli attack began with the destruction of the camp's electricity supply, which was established in 1965 and renovated in 1994. The sewer system, established in 1991, was also destroyed. The water system was also destroyed, it was established in 1963. The phone system was finally completed in the 1990s. That too was destroyed.

After the third or fourth day of the invasion, not one ambulance, not one fire truck, no humanitarian aid, or even journalists were allowed entry into the camp. For thirteen days, Jenin refugee camp was cut off from the world. It was on April 13 that the Israeli army allowed the Red Crescent and the Red Cross to recover the bodies.

Personnel from the Red Crescent came to my house and asked me to come and help identify bodies. I then realized that the Israeli army was dictating what areas rescue workers were allowed to go to and what areas were forbidden. On that day, we recovered fourteen bodies. They were decomposed, smelled horrid, and were covered with maggots. It was very difficult to identify them, the faces were darkened and the skin felt like plastic. It was as if they had plastic suits on. We did our best to write down the names of the victims and where they were found. Afterwards, we took them back to the hospital.

I consider these days like another diaspora for the people of Jenin, similar to their diaspora in 1948. I was only a child then. Can you imagine a full-scale invasion with tanks and warplanes unleashed on a small residential area whose size does not exceed 375 *dunums*, where 13,900 people live, of which 5,200 are children? Can you imagine the horror that the people must have felt when missiles began falling on their houses and killing them?

This is not the first time that the Israelis attacked Jenin refugee camp in the current uprising. They had earlier experiences, most notably, on February 28, 2002. They staged a three-day attack and were forced to pull out because of the intensity of the resistance. That's why when they invaded in April, they were well aware of the strength of the resistance and the unity among the fighters. The camp lost twenty-five fighters. The great majority of the dead and wounded, the cases of abuse, detentions, and arrests were among the civilians. Older people and children were the greatest victims.

The resistance would have continued longer if it weren't for the destruction of most of the camp. The resistance had great faith in justice and in God. The resistance was led by Abu Jandal, the leader of national security with the Palestinian Authority, as well as Ziad al-Amr, the head of Al-Aqsa Brigade, and Mahmud Tawalbe, the head of the Islamic Jihad movement. Also, the Islamic Movement Hamas was led by Muhammad al-Hilo. In addition, were people unaffiliated with any particular group, but they too fought for our just cause. The resistance used light weapons, such as M-16s, but most of the firearms were old rifles. There was a great deal of solidarity between the people and their fighters. People shared food and clothes with them.

The Israeli soldiers treated Palestinians in the most inhumane ways imaginable. When they arrested people, if they didn't kill them or haul them in, they would strip them completely naked and leave them in remote villages, miles from Jenin. Many, however, endured a worse fate than that. People were beaten to death, like Hosni Faed. Others were

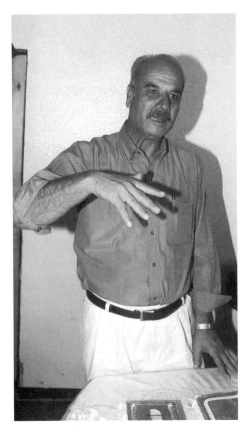

Abdelrazik Abu al-Hayjah

crushed under tanks, like Jamal al-Sabbagh, whose toes were the only part of his body not crushed. Ahmed Hamdouni was a seventy-two-year-old man, his house was bombed and caught on fire. He came running out with a bag of bread that he managed to salvage. Just as he emerged from his home, Israeli snipers shot him. They tied him and then they dragged him into a neighbor's home. That neighbor was handcuffed, and they were tied to the couch. In their house, he bled to death. Others were executed in the street after being snatched away from their families and children. There was Ifaf Dusuki. She came running to open the door for the soldiers, but they showered her with bullets the moment she opened the door. There was Raja Abu Sibah and Mariam al-Wishahe. These were all innocent people, women, elders and handicapped, whose deaths speak chapters about the Israeli conduct in Jenin.

During the invasion, people had great faith that we would emerge victorious. It is because they have faith in God. They believed in God and they do not question fate. Almost every family in Jenin had something to mourn. Some people had loved ones killed, others are missing, others in prison. Most homes were completely destroyed or damaged. It might not seem so bad that someone's house was damaged or destroyed, but with destroyed homes, everything is gone. Their possessions, their memories, their important documents, their life's savings, I mean everything. People here are nevertheless determined to rebuild their camp. The refugee camp is not a real homeland but people are so used having the tight community and are determined to stay with each other.

If Israel destroys the camp many times, the people of Jenin will rebuild it because with every Israeli attack, the people's courage and determination intensifies. The more Israel brutalizes Palestinians, the stronger their resistance shall be. Israel cannot resolve its problems by force. They have to understand that Palestinians' quest for freedom cannot be stopped. It is only human nature for people to resist, in order to regain their freedom. Palestinians are only demanding that Israel leave the areas they illegally occupied in 1967. This is only twenty-two percent of the original size of Palestine seized by Israel in 1948. The people of Jenin do not hate Israelis because their names are different or because their language is different. Nor do they hate them because they have anything against the Jewish religion. Israel is despised because they are the occupiers. And as long as they are occupiers, the resistance will go on.

The resistance could increase or decrease, but it will never die. If not during this generation, the people of Jenin and Palestine will gain their freedom through the will of coming generations. Why can't the Israelis understand that Palestinian freedom is imminent and spare both nations the bloodshed of many years to come? Israel cannot continue playing political games with the Palestinians—by stealing their land, robbing them of their holy city of Jerusalem, building new illegal settlements, and constructing new illegal bypass roads. It is not surprising that a Palestinian chooses to be a human bomb—continuously suffering injustice can do even more than that. The Palestinian resistance shall live as long as the occupation lives.

TESTIMONIES

INTERNATIONAL OBSERVERS

Jennifer Loewenstein

Jennifer Loewenstein is a senior lecturer at the University of Wisconsin-Madison School of Business. She has traveled and worked extensively in the Palestinian Occupied Territories. She is the author of "Banishment: The Palestinian Refugees of Lebanon" in Roane Carey's The New Intifada *(Verso, 2001). She lives and works in Madison, Wisconsin. Her comment is titled "The Most Humane Thing to Do."*

Dead bodies were laid out in the dirt beside the wrecked hospital in the Jenin refugee camp where workers with surgical masks over their faces waited to load them into open-backed trucks. The smell of death was so overpowering that children covered their faces with their shirts, and some of the journalists covered their mouths and noses with strips of cloth torn from articles of their clothing. A young man weeping uncontrollably into the arms of his friend stood near the bodies, and an old woman shouted through tears of rage, "Stop taking pictures!" A man smeared with blood from the bodies led her away.

I counted twenty-seven bodies here, behind the hospital. Emergency relief workers had just brought some of them from inside the devastated camp, though not all had yet been recovered. I watched as another group of men dug up more bodies from makeshift graves behind the hospital where some of the dead had been buried temporarily during the siege. The Israeli Army had prevented their families from giving them a proper burial. It also prevented medical relief and ambulances from coming into the camp. I interviewed the chief doctor at the Shifa Surgical Hospital in the city of Jenin and verified this information with three other doctors and ambulance drivers. No, there was no shortage of blood or oxygen in their hospital. Why? Because medical workers were not allowed in to help the wounded in the Jenin refugee camp. In fact, when the ambulance drivers attempted to go in anyway, IDF soldiers fired on them. Emergency food aid was allowed in only after the IDF left. I spoke to people from Save the Children and Medicins Sans Frontiers whose outrage at the situation could barely be contained.

I walked through Jenin that day and the scene was surreal. What had been a crowded refugee camp was now a wrecked, bulldozed mass of destruction unlike anything I had ever seen or even imagined. Between 13,000 and 14,000 people lost their homes and all of their possessions during the indecently named Operation Defensive Shield. Nothing is left of the former Jenin camp except ruins. The interior of the camp is a moonscape of rubble and dirt, flattened beyond recognition. A woman rummaging through a pile of concrete said to me that she couldn't even tell where her former home had been.

The houses along the perimeter of the camp are still standing in a semicircle. They have been so completely destroyed inside that no one could again live in them. Tank shells blew huge holes into the external walls, leaving gaping wounds that afforded one a view inside bedrooms, kitchens, and living areas of people's former lives. Broken glass lay scattered everywhere along with chunks of concrete that would fall randomly from the ceilings, many of which had holes in them from missiles and tank shells. Soldiers had in some instances burned family photographs. In one house, flour for making bread had been dumped on the kitchen floor along with all of the kitchenware. Soldiers had scribbled offensive graffiti inside the walls of many of the homes. In one, a Star of David with hateful words written in it filled up part of a living room wall. In another, a picture of the Dome of the Rock being blown up stained the wall of a staircase. On a bathroom door someone had scribbled in Hebrew, "If you need to take a piss, go upstairs." Upstairs was a child's bedroom. There was garbage strewn everywhere inside the houses where soldiers had taken over. The IDF had cut all electricity and water to the camp. In some of the houses soldiers had defecated inside refrigerators or kitchen pots and urinated into the sinks. In the camp mosque, the minaret loudspeaker used by the muezzin to call his people to prayer had been vandalized and defecated in.

Walking was unsafe in Jenin, whether you were outside picking your way through blasted blocks of cement and wire, or inside trying to step over destroyed furniture, scattered and torn clothing, or broken household items. A television set had been shot. The speakers of a stereo had bullets in them. "Are these appliances also considered terrorist?" I wondered.

I watched in horror as a small family shack at the edge of the camp burst into flames after a loud explosion. A missile fired from an American-made helicopter had not exploded when it landed in the house three days previously. The family mercifully escaped, but nothing remains of their belongings. Throughout the camp one could find spent ammunition, used bullets, tank shells, the remnants of missiles, and more—the fingerprints of Israel's crime. Worse, however, were those that were lying unexploded, half-hidden from view, waiting for the unsuspecting child to stumble across them—something that happened on a number of occasions.

Do not tell me that this was a humanely carried out military operation in defense of Israel. I was there. I spent two days and a night in Jenin's ruins immediately after the Israelis pulled out. I saw people desperately searching for remnants of their former lives. I heard people begging for information about loved ones killed, missing, or taken away to prison. I listened to a story, repeated to me several times by several different individuals, of four men who were summarily executed.

"Israeli soldiers tied the hands of four men behind their backs," I was told. "Then soldiers forced them to kneel beside a concrete wall. A few minutes later, soldiers fired bullets into the backs of their heads at close range."

I watched as children wandered aimlessly around the expanse of debris with expressionless, traumatized faces. I smelled the putrid smell of death coming from heaps of rubble from houses that had been demolished. These heavy concrete and block buildings had fallen to the ground, crushing their inhabitants. I still lack the words that can fully express the horror of what I saw.

Do not tell me that Israel was defending itself from "militants, terrorists, and gunmen" in Jenin. The Palestinians of Jenin were defending their own homes on their own land, a land that has been illegally occupied for 35 years. Israel has no legal or moral right to be on this land. It has no legal or moral right to murder people for opposing this occupation. It has no legal or moral right to keep building Jewish settlements on Palestinian land and to continue stealing the resources of this land. It has no legal or moral right to continue depriving this people of their basic humanity. But, for the record, the Palestinian people do have the right, under international law, to resist this barbaric occupation (UN General Assembly Resolution 42/159; 7 December 1987).

jloewenstein@hotmail.com

197

Riad Z. Abdelkarim, MD

Dr. Riad Z. Abdelkarim is a physician in Anaheim, California, and a founder of Kids In Need of Development, Education, and Relief (KINDER-USA), an American non-profit organization working on behalf of Palestinian children. He is also the Regional Communications Director for CAIR, the Council on American-Islamic Relations. In addition he is a board member of American Muslims for Jerusalem. He was born, raised, and educated in the United States. Dr. Abdelkarim titles his comments: "A Day in the Jenin Refugee Camp: Questions, Images and Sounds."

After visiting the Jenin refugee camp, I feel ashamed to be part of a world that has allowed such a monstrous crime to occur. All of the pictures on the internet, the images on satellite television, the thousands and thousands of words already written about this crime, my previous witnessing of the destruction in Khan Yunus, Rafah, and Bethlehem—did not prepare me adequately for the scenes of devastation and despair that I witnessed.

Upon entering the camp and passing a huge mound of rubble—the remnants of a building—a horrible, foul, spine-tingling odor struck me. It was the smell of death. We have all heard about it—seen survivors of this massacre talk about it—but I somehow did not expect it to still be present one and a half weeks after the Israeli pullout. Yet there it was, greeting the dozens upon dozens of foreign and non-governmental organization (NGO) delegations walking through the camp. Nobody knows how many are buried underneath, but there is no question that life was extinguished below this mound of rubble.

Camp residents were walking around as if in a trance, still clearly not able to comprehend—or accept—the wholesale destruction of their homes. It was as if the entire camp had been drugged.

Everywhere I went, there were stories of terror, stories of executions, stories of huge D-9 Caterpillar bulldozers that would knock down a home with a single push—with entire families still inside. There was a story of the eighty-five-year-old partially blind man whom I visited in a Jenin hospital. He had been struck by shrapnel from an Apache helicopter rocket fired at his home. There was a story of a young man who lost his right leg and part of his right hand when his home was shelled as well. There was the eighteen-year-old boy who was killed in front of his home. We sat to offer our condolences to his uncle and cousin. Then I learned that the boy's mother was shot—also in front of the house—a mere 24 hours later. She too had died. This was a double tragedy.

There were stories of ambulances prevented from entering to evacuate the injured and dead, and stories of women being virtually strip-searched by soldiers before being allowed to escape the camps. We also were told of a young man who was used as a "human shield" by the crew of an APC searching a school. They would open each classroom door and push him inside, to test for any booby traps. An old man told me he had lived in his home in the camp for 50 years. "What will I do now? Where will I go?" He walked away, stooped over, with a tear welling up in his eye.

There was the story of the woman who said she had received donations of food, but had no gas or electricity with which to cook them. I heard many stories of burned-out bodies of victims pulled from the rubble, days after they were killed. There were stories of curfews and snipers. And finally, the horrifying story of the mosque whose loudspeaker was used as a toilet by Israeli soldiers.

Walking down the dusty road of Jenin, I saw graffiti scrawled in English on a wall, "Occupation is the real terrorism."

Four or five young boys were playing in the dirt next to a heap of rubble. "What are you doing?" I asked. "We are building a tent, since our home was destroyed."

I saw home after home with significant structural damage, but not totally destroyed—a wall or two or three missing. In the US, such homes would be declared unsafe and sealed off. Not here. A few metal rods were used to support the structure, and children played on what was once a balcony. This was not safe at all.

Farther down the road, an old man sat on the rubble next to his home, staring into the distance, seemingly oblivious to the camp's visitors, and indeed to everything else around him. A penny for his thoughts . . .

For as far as the eye could see (several football fields), not a single home was left undamaged or fully intact. The earthquake analogy was apt. The difference: no search and rescue teams, no sniffing dogs looking for survivors, no real coordinated international effort to remove the rubble.

At the camp's United Nations medical clinic, I saw evidence of deliberate destruction and looting. I saw bullet holes in a scale used to weigh babies. A grenade tossed into the reception area, with holes all over the ceiling and walls. The electric motor to a dental chair device stolen. A sterilizing autoclave destroyed. Bullet holes in a door marked with a sign that read, "Pregnant Women's Care."

I run into a fifty-something, blonde American woman volunteering for a local medical NGO. She speaks to us in Arabic. When I mention that I'm from the United States, she responds in Arabic: "So, you are from the 'head of the snake!'" She tells me she lived in Berkeley some time ago.

As I leave the camp's Ground Zero, I feel an uncomfortable mixture of sadness, grief, anger, and shame. I also feel guilt. My tax dollars helped pay for these bullets, these Apache helicopter death-ships, these monstrous Caterpillar bulldozers. When I tell camp survivors that I'm from the United States, I am ashamed. I, too, am responsible for this. Walking around with my video camera and digital still camera, I feel as if I am participating in some grotesque, macabre ritual.

I spent last night in the Jenin area. I slept about two hours, then could not sleep anymore. My head still hurts. My nose still recalls that horrible odor. My mind keeps replaying these images and these stories. And my heart continues to ache—mostly for the people of Jenin, but also for what we used to call humanity.

Riad Zuhdi@aol.com

Kathy Kelly

Kathy Kelly of Chicago helped initiate Voices in the Wilderness, a campaign to end the UN/US sanctions against Iraq. During April 15-17, 2002, she visited the Jenin Camp, along with six companions. Their effort was organized by the International Solidarity Movement immediately following the Israeli army's "Operation Enduring Force" attack on the camp. Kathy Kelly's comment is titled "Searching for the Truth in Jenin."

On April 17, we entered the Jenin camp for a third time, accompanied by Thawra.

We had met Thawra the night we first entered Jenin. She came into the crowded, makeshift clinic organized by Palestinian Medical Relief Committee workers, cradling Ziad, an 18-day-old infant born on the first night of the attack against Jenin. Like most of the young Palestinian workers volunteering with the Medical Relief Committee, she wore *hijab* and blue jeans.

She had slept very little in the previous ten days, working constantly to assist refugees from the camp. Her fiancé, Mustafa, was missing. Many people whispered to us that they were sure he was killed inside the Jenin camp, but that Thawra still hoped he was alive.

Today was Thawra's first chance to find out what had happened to her home. She and her family lived on the first floor of a three story building. Mustafa lived on the third floor.

Entering the camp, we noticed spray-painted images that Israeli soldiers must have made the night before. On the entrance gate to one building, in blue paint, was a stick figure image of a little girl holding the Israeli flag. Next to it was a Star of David with an exclamation point inside the star.

We passed Israeli soldiers preparing to leave the house they had occupied. Five soldiers and an APC positioned themselves to protect a soldier as he walked out of the house carrying the garbage. "Five soldiers and an APC to take out the trash," said Jeff. "That's a sure sign that something is radically wrong."

Most of the homes at the edge of the camp are somewhat intact, although doors, windows, and walls are badly damaged by tank shells and Apache bullets. Each home that we entered had been ransacked. Drawers, desks and closets were emptied. Refrigerators were turned over, light fixtures pulled out of the walls, clothing torn.

I thought of the stories women told me, earlier that morning, about Israeli soldiers entering their homes with large dogs that sniffed at the children as neighbors fled from explosions, snipers, fires and the nightmare chases of bulldozers.

As we climbed higher, entering the demolished center of the camp where close to 100 housing units have been flattened by Israeli Defense Forces, we heard snipers shooting at a small group of men who had come to pull bodies from the rubble. Covered with dust and sweat, and seemingly oblivious to the gunshots, the men, all residents from the camp, pursued the grim task. With pickaxes and shovels, they dug a mass grave.

They pulled four bodies out of the rubble, including that of a small child. Little boys stood still, silently watching. Several days earlier, one of the many soldiers who stopped us as we walked into Jenin City told us there were no children in the camp during the attack. This was a lie. But now I wonder if it may have been a strange truth. The concerned frowns on the little boys' faces were those of hardened men.

An older boy, perhaps 10 or 11 years old, helped carry his father's corpse to the mass grave.

Jeff sat down on a rock and shook his head. "After September 11, I drove toward New York City. On the highway carloads of volunteer firemen from all over the country sped past me. They wanted to help at Ground Zero. Here in Jenin, bullets paid for by US taxpayers are being fired on people simply trying to bury their dead."

A family trudged single file, silently, uphill through the debris, carrying their belongings on their heads. Their faces were wracked with grief. One woman carried an infant in her arms. No one spoke. At the top of the hill, in front of a house that was still somewhat intact, a large family was seated as though posed for a family photograph, surrounded by devastation.

Thawra led us to what was once her home. The house was still standing, but every other house in the area was completely demolished. She quickly collected some clothes, then went to the third floor and returned holding Mustafa's blue jeans in her arms. Her eyes welled with tears. Had she lost all hope of finding Mustafa?

Outside Thawra's home, we met eight-year-old Ahmad. He had found six shiny, small bullets which he showed to his neighbor, Muhammad Abdul Khalil. Muhammad is a forty-two-year-old mason, also trained as an accountant. Having worked in Brazil and Jordan, he now speaks four languages. In Spanish, he told me that he built many kitchens in this area. Muhammad nodded kindly at Ahmad.

A few feet away, Hitan, age twenty, and Noor, age sixteen, dug through the debris with their bare hands to retrieve some few belongings. Hitan found a favorite jacket, torn and covered with dust. She fingered the pockets, then set it aside. Noor laughed as she unearthed a matching pair of shoes. Then Hitan saw the edge of a textbook and the sisters began vigorously digging and tugging until they pulled out five battered and unusable books. Noor held up her public health textbook. Hitan clutched *The History of Islamic Civilization.*

"You see these girls, they are laughing and seem playful," said, Muhammad, again speaking in Spanish. "It is, you know, a coping mechanism. How else can they manage what they feel?" Hitan stood and pointed emphatically at the small hole she and Noor had dug. "You know," she exclaims, "underneath here, there are four televisions and two computers! All gone. Finished."

Thawra stared sadly, then persisted in her search for information about Mustafa.

I asked Muhammad if he knew a man sorting through a huge mound of rubble next to where we stood. "He is my cousin," said Muhammad. "That was our home. He wants to find his passport or his children's documents." Muhammad's cousin then sat down on top of the heap that was once his home, holding his head in his hands.

An army surveillance plane flew overhead.

"We are clear," said Muhammad. "We are not animals. We are people with hearts and blood, just like you. I love my son. I want the life for my family. What force do we have here? Is this a force?" He pointed to the wreckage all around us. "Do we have the atomic bomb?" "Do we have anthrax?"

As we walked away, Jeff pointed at another bone sticking out of the debris. We stepped gingerly around it. Thawra dipped down to pick up a veil lying on the ground, then she paused a moment and placed it over the bone.

kkelly@igc.org, info@vitw.org

Ramzy Baroud

Ramzy Baroud is a Palestinian-American journalist. He is the editor of PalestineChronicle.com, *a leading Palestinian online publication. His English columns are published, translated, or reviewed in many print and online publications around the world. His Arabic columns are published weekly by London's* Al-Arab International *newspaper. This piece is titled "In Critical Condition: Speaking with Fighters from Jenin."*

Mahmoud is a polite young man, or appears to be. It's difficult to determine what he had possibly looked like in the past. But now he has very little flesh to support his exposed bones, very pale, with a skeleton face and a sharp nose. Mahmoud lies in a hospital, unable to talk or to walk. He usually eats through a small tube in his nose. He can only respond to the greetings of his visitors by blinking with his eyes and nodding his head a little. The twenty-two-year-old is in critical condition. A bullet penetrated his throat and lungs and is lodged in his back. He lingers between death and permanent disability.

I violated the serenity of Mahmoud's room in a Jordanian hospital as I entered with my heavy bag, recorders, small microphone, cameras, and laptop. Initially I felt out of place in this large room where several other wounded Palestinian boys and young men lay, some crying out in pain and others unconscious.

A few moments later I felt at home. Now their pain was mine, and their faces reminded me of my friends who also wasted away. They had started out fighting for freedom and ending up in a lonely hospital, fighting for their lives.

Mahmoud is from the Jenin refugee camp, one of many resistance heroes whose stories are told by the camp's survivors as they sleep among the ruins of their homes. The young man is still handsome with a dignified look. He cannot talk, although he tries. But no words come out, just air. Using nods of his head and gestures made with his gentle eyes, he persistently tries to communicate.

Mahmoud's older brother is also a refugee from Jenin. He is a tall, handsome young man who stands by his brother's bedside, thanking the few visitors who come to see the Jenin hero. The older brother was in a celebrating mood. For the first time since he had been shot, Mahmoud had eaten. I was lucky to be part of this historic moment. A few other men stood nearby and congratulated the older brother. "God willing," one said, "some day he'll walk and talk." The older brother agreed. Yet he seemed sad. He knew that this statement was an exaggeration, an effort to give Mahmoud courage.

Mahmoud was not a member of any Palestinian faction, but a fighter who took to the streets to defend Jenin when the Israelis attacked.

Mahmoud's brother hesitated to answer my questions. He feared that any information he provided would reach the Israelis who would arrest Mahmoud at the border. I told him that I would change the names and would not mention the hospital's name or location.

"Mahmoud is a resistance hero," his brother said. "He was shot in the leg and returned two days later to the battlefield, where he was shot right in the neck."

"We are four brothers and six sisters. Mahmoud is the only unmarried brother. He stayed to help our parents care for the others. He was carrying the family on his shoulders. We helped as much as we could, but he was the provider," he said.

I then turned to Mahmoud, who followed the conversation with his large eyes. A few tears had gathered, and I could see a shade of red in his eyes.

Mahmoud's brother continued to speak, as he gently checked that Mahmoud was fully covered. "You know," he said, "Mahmoud wrote to me (as he cannot talk) and told me, 'the chief of staff of the Israeli army, Shaul Mofaz, was in the helicopter that chased me and gunned me down.' I tried to visualize the head of the Israeli army chasing behind this frail body in the impoverished streets of the Jenin refugee camp. Mahmoud now writes, 'Once I am well, I will return to defend the camp.'"

Two Palestinian men, also visiting Mahmoud, asked me to convey his story to the world so that someone might help him. "They say that the only place that can treat such cases is Austria," one of the visitors said. "Do you know anyone in Austria?"

"I don't," I replied. "But I promise I will do all that I can." I was aware of how little I could do.

I learned that the Israelis refused three times to allow the ambulance carrying Mahmoud to enter Jordan. The unconscious young man was searched time and again. Days later, after the ambulance driver begged for the sake of his patient, he was let into Jordan.

"Hospitals in Jenin are full of wounded," his brother said. "There is no space left to treat more."

"Our family's home in Jenin was shelled and is half-burnt," said the brother. "It's full of holes and could fall any moment. The rest of the family is still living in the ailing house. They have no place to go. They are not willing to leave anyway. The camp is our home, we belong there, until the day Palestine is free."

I asked to take a photo. Other patients—an old man who lost his home and shop in Jenin and is staying with his wounded wife at the hospital, a wounded fighter who told me that his greatest regret was not being able to fight for the camp until the end—volunteered to pose in the photo as well. They all smiled and I snapped the photo.

I ascended the stairs of the hospital's second floor. "Tell the world what has happened to us," a wounded man called out to me.

"The world knows nothing," I thought.

I kept on walking, hauling my bulky bag, and carrying in my heart Mahmoud's face, peaceful and dying.

editor@PalestineChronicle.com

Marilyn Robinson

Marilyn Robinson is a member of the Colorado Campaign for Middle East Peace. She is one of three members of a group who joined international observers in solidarity with Palestinians nonviolently resisting Israel's illegal military occupation. Her comment is titled "Nawal and the Purple Flower Trees."

Leaving Jenin was heartbreaking. Families I had stayed with kept hugging and kissing me, pleading with me not to go. "Stay," they would say, "you are my second mamma," said Nawal, a strikingly beautiful, young Palestinian woman of nineteen who had become my adopted daughter almost immediately after I first met her.

She was one of the many volunteers who worked at the Medical Relief Center in Jenin Refugee Camp. She lived in the camp. She had so little but would have freely given me everything she had. We shared many moments together.

We walked down the scarred, pot holed streets of Jenin and the camp. We passed leftover memories of buildings that had once been homes, children's centers, and hospital additions under-construction before the Israeli military attacked. The homes of Nawal's friends had gaping holes in their walls reminiscent of giant mouths wailing in silence. Holes from rocket bombs and missiles, gunshot holes, and holes from shrapnel perforate fence walls, their homes, and their doors. Interior walls, now visible from the street, still held the framed photographs of the families who must still live here because there is nowhere else to go.

Those families stood at their doorways and bid welcome. They offered tea or Arabic coffee that was already prepared as though they had been magically awaiting my arrival. They thanked me over and over again for coming, for being there, for being witness to their stories, and to witness the wanton, barbaric destruction of their homes and land. They pleaded, "Please tell America what happened here. Tell them we are not terrorists. Tell them we want to live in peace, but Israel, Sharon, and Bush will not let us."

Their convictions stand. They stand the test of time. They will not relent on the truth and its convictions. "Live free or die" was spraypainted on one of the walls still standing in the camp—the motto on the

207

New Hampshire license plate I well remember seeing when I lived there. I recall how people in New Hampshire used to question what it really meant. The people of Jenin camp know what it means. To live free or die is no question, it is a moral, a value, a code of honor. It is a belief that will remain etched on the walls of Jenin camp and in the hearts of the Palestinian people of Jenin camp and the West Bank.

When I prepared to leave Jenin, there were many heartfelt good byes to say. I had adopted Nawal, as I had so many. But she was special. At that moment she was very special with her dark, sad, yet loving eyes boring into my soul. I held her hand and said, "It must be so difficult to make a friend and then, they leave." She said no one had been like me, I had adopted her. Not any of her friends had two mothers like she did. She was lucky. The stars had shined on her when I came into her life.

She said she would not forget me. She handed me a small photo that I will treasure the rest of my life. We had seen the horrors left from the invasion, yet she remembered my delight as I marveled at the trees with their light purple flowers. She said that she will remember how I danced in the street of the purple flower trees, singing "You Are My Sunshine" to her.

When I got into the taxi with the others, ready for our journey, I turned to look for her. She was standing there smiling as she had done much of the time I was with her. We blew each other kisses. A bond had grown between us. Nawal and the purple flower trees will remain waiting for my return.

Uri Avnery

Long-time Israeli peace activist Uri Avnery is a founding member of Gush Shalom and the Israeli Council for Israeli-Palestinian Peace. Avnery has authored numerous books and articles on the Israel-Palestine conflict. This commentary piece is titled "The Truth Lies Under the Rubble."

There is full agreement between all those who were in the Jenin refugee camp on only one thing. A week after the end of the fighting, foreign journalists and IDF soldiers, UN representatives and hired hacks in the Israeli media, members of the welfare organizations and government propagandists all report that a terrible stench of decomposing bodies lingers everywhere.

Apart from that there is no agreement on anything. The Palestinians speak about a massacre amounting to a second Sabra and Shatila. The IDF speak about hard fighting, in which "the most humane army in the world" did not intentionally hurt even one single civilian.

So what is the truth? The simple answer is: nobody knows. Nobody can possibly know. The truth lies buried under the debris, and it smells atrociously.

Some facts, however, are incontestable. They are sufficient for drawing conclusions.

First: During two weeks of fighting, the IDF did not allow any journalist, Israeli or foreign, into the camp. Even after the fighting had died down, no journalist was let in. The pretext was that the life of the journalists would be endangered. But they did not ask the army to save them. They were quite ready to risk their lives, as journalists and photographers do in every war.

Simple common sense would hold that if one forcibly denies access to journalists, one has something to hide.

Second: During the fighting and afterwards, ambulances and rescue teams were not allowed to get close. Those that tried to approach were shot at. The result was that the wounded bled to death in the streets, even if they had relatively light injuries. This is a war crime, a manifestly illegal order, over which the black flag of illegality flies. Under Israeli law, and even more so under international law and conventions to which Israel is a party, soldiers are forbidden to obey such an order.

It makes no difference whether civilians or armed men, one person or a hundred, died under these circumstances. As a method of warfare it is inhuman.

Some journalists justified this method in advance when they alleged that they had seen "with their own eyes" Palestinian ambulances carrying arms. Even if there was such an incident, it would not justify the use of such methods in any circumstances. In fact, until now, only one instance of an ambulance on a military mission has been verified: Israeli journalists proudly reported that undercover Israeli soldiers used an ambulance in order to approach a house in which a "wanted person" was hiding.

Third: Even after the end of the fighting, several days later, heavy equipment and rescue teams were not allowed in to remove the debris and corpses, or perhaps save people still alive under the ruins.

The pretext was again that the corpses could be mined. So what? If foreign and local teams want to risk their lives for this noble purpose, why should the army prevent them from doing so?

Fourth: During all the days of fighting, no one was allowed to bring in medications, water and food. I myself took part in a mass march of Israeli peace activists who tried, after the fighting was over, to accompany a convoy of trucks carrying such supplies to the camp. The trucks were allowed, so it seemed, to pass the road-block which stopped us—but it later became apparent that the supplies were unloaded in an army camp and only four trucks could reach their destination.

What does all this indicate? An objective person could only draw the conclusion that the army wanted to prevent the entrance of eye-witnesses into the camp at any price. The army knew that this would give rise to rumors about a terrible massacre, but preferred this to the disclosure of the truth. If one takes such extreme measures to hide something, one cannot complain about the rumors.

What is the height of cynicism? When one blocks free access to a place, and then argues that no one has the right to say what happened there, because he has not seen it with his own eyes.

The most damning evidence about what happened is the fact that immediately after the end of the fighting, top government and army officials started to discuss ways of preventing a shock reaction in Israel and abroad once the facts became known. This was no secret discussion, it was held in public, in the media talk shows. All of us heard.

The decisions made were extremely effective in Israel, and extremely ineffective abroad. I happened to be in England when the news finally broke. They filled the first page of every important British newspaper. The front-page headline in the Times was "Inside the Camp of Death." Underneath was a giant photo and a report by a star war correspondent, who wrote that in all the wars she had covered, such as Bosnia, Kosovo, Chechnya and others, she had never seen such a terrible sight as this. In almost all European countries the reaction was the same.

In Israel, however, the government propaganda machine, in which all the media are now voluntarily integrated, did everything possible to prepare the public in advance. It was said beforehand that the Palestinians were about to spread a horrible lie, that they were ready to heap dead bodies (from where?) in the streets. It got almost to the point of saying that the Palestinians had blown up their houses over their families in order to create a blood libel.

The IDF did "clean" part of the camp, removing the bodies and ordering the ruins somewhat, and that is where compliant journalists and innocent foreign visitors were brought. There they met calm, humane officers who assured them that there had not been any massacre. After all, only a tiny part of the camp had been destroyed, so-and-so many yards by so-and-so many yards, nothing really. It all reminds one of the methods of certain regimes.

The result is that again a huge gap was created between Israelis and the rest of the world. Around the world, many were horrified that Jews, of all people, were capable of doing such things. Jews were again confirmed in their belief that all goyim (non-Jews) are anti-Semites.

I hope that there will be a serious international inquiry, and that the truth—whatever it may be—will emerge. But if even a part of the rumored atrocity is confirmed, a question will be asked: What was the intention? Why did the civilian and military leadership decide to deal with the Jenin camp like this?

The only answer I can come up with is that in Jenin the Palestinians decided to stand up and fight. The rape of Jenin was intended to send a message to the Palestinians: This will be the lot of everyone who resists the IDF. Also, it could cause a Deir Yassin-style mass flight.

Only a fool would believe that this will end the resistance to the occupation.

avnery@actcom.co.il

William J. Thomson, PhD

Dr. Thomson is on the faculty of the University of Michigan-Dearborn, where he teaches in the areas of clinical psychology and nonviolence/violence. He is also a clinical psychologist in private practice, with specific expertise in the treatment of psychological trauma. He has been involved in anti-war and nonviolence activities since the Vietnam era.

On Tuesday April 23 2002, a group of some 25 Palestinians and internationals traveled from Jerusalem to Jenin camp. By bus, taxi and foot, we arrived at the camp at mid morning, having encountered no Israeli military along the way. The lack of exposure to the IDF was strictly a function of the skill of our Palestinian guides, as the city and camp remain surrounded.

In the camp we heard a succession of horrible stories. Civilians were shot in cold blood, and then first aid supplies were placed on the body to make it appear that the IDF had rendered assistance. One victim was repeatedly run over by a tank, crushing his body into an unrecognizable mash. Both men and women were ordered to strip completely—two elderly men who refused were summarily executed. The soldiers stole telephones, money, jewelry—anything of value that could be carried.

The scene of the devastation was horrifying. Within an area of approximately 500 yards by 500 yards, there was not a single structure remaining. Even the remnants of houses were pulverized beyond recognition. All that remained were several mounds of dust-covered rubble between one to two stories high. Residents attempted to identify where they had lived by finding a familiar blanket, bucket, or toy. The empty area was surrounded with a perimeter of structures that were missing walls and were in danger of imminent collapse. Residents were digging through the rubble with their bare hands in search of corpses and any salvageable items. On the day we were there, five bodies were discovered, including that of an infant.

Clearly all of the houses were not fully occupied during the attack, but it is equally clear that the number of deaths in this area must have been considerable.

The stories we heard are distressingly similar, differing only in details. According to Dr. Muhammad Abu-Ghali, a pediatrician who is Director of Jenin Hospital, only 102 injuries were reported, due to the ruthless efficiency with which the IDF went about its gruesome task. One young injured boy was Asad Faisal Awad (10), who had two broken legs, missing toes, a missing arm, was blind and on a ventilator to assist with his labored breathing. His father was praying for his death, a death, which, we were later informed, had in fact occurred during our return to Jerusalem.

A child in the camp handed me a piece of ordinance which an expert in Ann Arbor identified as either an M-203 grenade or a 40mm chain gun missile fired by an Apache helicopter. In either case, we are talking about a rather indiscriminate weapon—much like a hand grenade, which if fired into a typical concrete block room would likely kill everyone inside, collapse the ceiling, and significantly damage the walls. It is a crude, imprecise weapon. Perhaps it was just such a grenade that led to the death of Asad. It should also be noted that the ordinance contained both English and Hebrew markings, which led my expert friend to believe with more than 90% certainty that the weapon had originated in the United States, paid for by our tax dollars.

As a clinical psychologist with a special expertise in trauma, I was impressed by the mood of the people in the camp. Clearly they had been dealt a terrible blow, and yet the flags of Palestine were on display, and people were going about the business of recovery. One woman was preparing a meal near the edge of an open wall that had once been the side of her home. But perhaps the most striking example of recovery was the following: In the home of Um Sulhi an internal wall had been knocked down by Israeli soldiers as they were moving from home to home searching for "terrorists." However, in this home, the wall was already repaired, and a painting had been produced on the wall. In the midst of incredible destruction, there was now a beautiful work of art!

As I have found typical in refugee camps at various places around the world, as soon as we arrived in the camp we were surrounded by children. We asked one bright and beautiful Palestinian girl, Shairma (11), what she wanted to be when she grew up. "There is no hope here. I want to be a martyr." Another child, Eyad (10), said, "I want to resist, I don't want to go to school"—understandable, but very concerning sentiments.

The ray of hope comes from a brilliant Palestinian therapist, Dr.

Nadera Shalhoub-Kevorkian, who over several hours of conversation with these children was able to instill the desire to return to school. In fact, Shairma and Eyad accepted the responsibility of gathering their compatriots for a play/art therapy session arranged for after school the next day. So we have a small success, but there are far too few Dr. Naderas and way, way too many Shairmas and Eyads.

wthomson@umich.edu

Trevor Baumgartner

Trevor Baumgartner traveled to Palestine as a participant in the International Solidarity Movement. He has studied and taught at June Jordan's Poetry for the People program at UC Berkeley, and currently teaches special education in Brooklyn, New York. Searching for hope amid the devastation, Trevor Baumgartner titles his piece "Jenin Means Garden."

"Did you see the people under the stones? Did you see them? Did you see the children shot in the school? Did you see them? Did you see my brother killed by an Apache helicopter? Did you see him? Did you see this what Israel calls 'life'? Can you see this life?"
— *Ghada, a resident of Mukhayim Jenin, 56 years old.*

A grandmother in a white head scarf and an elegantly embroidered turquoise gown clutches a case of water and crawls up and over slabs of cinder block and stucco. She's trying to find a place to store this water, supplied by local relief organizations. As she shoves them through a prison bar mesh of snarled rebar, I'm struck by her resolve. Her trembling but unbroken spirit. Her steadfast human will drives her body and keeps her in her home, Palestine—her living room, even though she's in the dead center of a major ethnic "cleanse," or what IDF soldiers call "purification."

When the wind picks up just right and washes over my face, I find myself engulfed by the scent of dead bodies. I've never tasted this smell before, but somehow I just know. There's nothing like the smell of a rotting heart. Nothing.

Walking into the camp, a local points to a patch of freshly turned earth. "They bury seven people there," he says. "They" being the IDF, who steadily deny everything they did here, as their strict adherence to "purity of arms" would never permit them to do anything as repugnant as digging and filling mass graves. But it's been shown on the news, and in the papers, and seen first hand by thousands of people, and no attempt at falsification, and no cowardly "fact-finding" team can change this truth.

I can't get used to this place—a luxury only few can afford. The devastation is absolute. I find myself just wandering in complete bewilderment through the pathways people have tramped in the rubble. Yesterday I stopped to tie my shoelace, right in the middle of somebody's family room. And the family was there next to me. A young girl tugged the tattered half of a photo from the dust and showed it to her father.

"What can I say to them?" Fatima, a local volunteer with the Union of Palestinian Medical Relief Committees (UPMRC), asks. "How can I ask the people here if their children want to come and play with us?" The UPMRC was attempting to organize a makeshift children's center, because an average of one person per day has been injured by unexploded bombs, and they thought it necessary to get young people away from this minefield.

"What are we supposed to do with this?" Fatima wonders out loud. Indeed, any "relief" we are capable of providing pales in comparison to the actual needs here. People are digging through an entire city block's worth of rubble with their bare hands—literally. Imagine a random group of untrained volunteers trying to "clean up" the wreckage that used to be the World Trade Center. That's the scale of devastation here—in fact, it's worse, because the number of displaced, in proportion, is astronomically higher.

This is not simply about counting the dead and displaced. It's about respect for human life. Whereas the US immediately rallied support for a war around the world, as well as a full-scale relief effort in New York, here a piddly UN "fact-finding" team can't even worm their way into this refugee camp, let alone use any machinery to uncover those men, women and children buried alive. What "facts" they'd be trying to find is another bewildering matter altogether, as everybody—everybody—knows who did what to whom. The treatment of the refugees in Jenin is pathological and utterly despicable. And we all bear some responsibility for it. They've been refugees for over fifty years, and many of them are now doubly displaced. Yet most of us look away in silence.

"We do not want your tears," Fatima explains. "We want you to do something."

These are not a pitiable people. They've spent their years building a fierce and proud community. In the face of intense and forced isolation. "No one here lives for personal achievement," Ibrahim explains, and he goes on to say that all the political and resistance groups coalesce here, despite radically differing ideologies. "We fought the soldiers back four times before they brought the Apaches."

"There's no way to compare the weapons," Shadi says. "We have only 120 guns in the whole camp, and they have tanks and Apaches and F-16s and bulldozers. If they don't bring the Apache, we will win . . . because we have faith in the land, but they just come to fight."

The stories of the strength of Mukhayim ("camp" in Arabic) Jenin are gaining legendary status. "The soldiers cry when they come to Jenin," many folks are proud to say. They are clear about making distinctions between resisting outside aggression/occupation and general terrorism. They are equally clear that everyday they survive terrorism from a state with nuclear capabilities.

Jenin will flower again, Shadi says, because "everybody here has the same goal." What is that goal, I ask.

"*Hurriya.*" It means freedom.

dromedary@graffiti.net

Susan Abulhawa

Susan Abulhawa is a freelance writer and activist based in Philadelphia. She has published numerous essays relating to the Palestine/Israel conflict. Susan is also the founder of a children's charity, which can be found at www.PlaygroundsForPalestine.org. "A New Face on an Old Situation" is the title of this piece.

I felt a gentle tap as I stood filming residents recover two more corpses from beneath the rubble at Jenin's ground zero. One was the body of an infant, the other a man, perhaps her father. I turned to find Fatima, a tall slender girl of ten years with a sweet disposition and a shy smile.

Fatima was one of several hundred children who gathered at the Palestinian Red Crescent Society to take part in a "day of recovery" for the children of Jenin. With limited resources, residents gathered the children from the camp for organized play—a small effort to comfort hundreds of tiny souls who lived through ten days of unrelenting terror.

Behind her beautiful smile, I could see that Fatima had seen far too much death in her young life, as she was unperturbed by the grisly spectacle of bodies being pulled from the rubble of a home she probably passed every day of her life. Indeed all the children seemed 'normal' on the surface. But the pictures they drew and the stories they told betrayed the profound tragedy they lived each day.

Iman, a deaf and mute little girl, drew a picture of a bloodied old man lying on the ground in front of a tank with the Star of David painted on it. Above him, she drew a helicopter firing missiles on a burning home. In the corner of her drawing was a girl with tears running down her face. I learned later that her grandfather was killed and his body left on the ground. Little Iman, unable to speak or hear, could feel the shaking of her home when it was fired upon by helicopter gunships. She could see and feel the panic of her mother and family. She watched her father get carted off in blindfolds and handcuffs. It is three weeks later and his whereabouts are still unknown. She saw her grandfather dead—his walking cane loyally still by his side. Iman is only seven years old.

Their wounds are bigger than me and any hurt I've ever known. Yet they still smile and play. When I left, there were still children who had no idea where their parents were. In homes where the IDF took up camp, entire families were packed into one room with little to no food or water for days. Samer, 8, told me that a soldier let him go to the bathroom only after he wet his pants. Aisha, 5, has not uttered a single word in three weeks. Amjad, 13, lost his life's savings that was in a wooden box he used to save up for a new bike. Khalid, 12, lost his father, three uncles and one cousin. Hiba, 4, huddled on the first floor of their home while helicopters rocketed the top two floors. I don't know how the spirit of a child survives here. But it does.

The day I spent talking to the children was my second day in the refugee camp. Already, I had witnessed the recovery of three corpses. The body of the infant exposed Israel's lies that no children were killed. I taped it. But I didn't see any other cameras there. In fact, there was little international presence in the camp. During my time there, I saw only three people from the Red Cross. Mostly, the activity of the camp came from its residents, who were walking around in a disbelieving daze, as though they were pacing through a vacuum in time, unable to comprehend past, present or future. One woman stood on a flat surface screaming curses at Ariel Sharon. She told me she was standing where her bedroom used to be. She had no children, no husband and no family. She just stood there, her emotions vacillating between angry curses and despairing tears.

On my third day in the camp, a British search and rescue team was dispatched after reports surfaced of people still alive under the rubble. I waited with hundreds of onlookers while they dug and searched for nine hours. Nothing. There were some ID papers and I spotted a human ulna (arm bone).

Fatima took me to a mosque on a hill where snipers had been positioned. The place was trashed and sprayed with Hebrew graffiti. From the roof of the mosque, you could survey the awesome devastation. Several people just looked out in silence. Two young boys, whose faces were still painted from the morning play at the Red Crescent, played with toy cars while burning cigarettes dangled from their young lips.

In the basement soldiers turned what was once a kindergarten into a big toilet—flies buzzed over their excrement inside the children's desks and on their toys. They had used pages from the Quran as toilet paper. On a mural of children's faces, soldiers had carved holes in the wall where eyes were once painted.

I asked Fatima what she wanted when she grew up. With an eerie cynicism of lost innocence, she challenged my assumption that she would not be killed before growing up. Then she rattled off a list of political and human rights goals, such as freedom and a Palestinian state." I asked again: "What do you want *just* for Fatima?"

She paused. "I want a doll house with little furniture inside. Have you ever seen one? I saw it in a picture."

I think of that simple wish and feel ashamed to live in relative comfort. I am haunted by the faces of lost innocence. The face that visits me most is that of Khalid, an asthmatic twelve-year-old boy who watched his father, stripped to his underwear, get shot in the back and then be crushed under the tread of a tank. He could barely breathe in the dust that pervaded the ruins. And his mother, searching for Khalid's nebulizer, found, instead, the shoe her husband was wearing when he was crushed. I shall never forget her face, her tears, nor Khalid's wheezing hell.

I went to Jenin to bear witness, to ease my own guilt for being spared, and to give what I could. In truth, I was the one who received lessons from their boundless resilience, kindness, and pride. When I left, a part of me remained there. I fell in love with Jenin. It is a place where unyielding toughness exists in perfect harmony with tenderness so tender it is humbling.

Though the heroism of Jenin's fighters may be perverted by propaganda, history will bow to these lightly armed men who fought until their last breath with an indomitable will and held off a mighty foe for ten days—four days longer than five armies were able to do in the past. They are true sons of the land. Having walked in the wake of what they died trying to prevent, I am changed.

sjabulhawa@aol.com

Dedrick Muhammad

Dedrick Muhammad is an African-American human rights activist based in Harlem. Currently Dedrick Muhammad is completing his Masters of Arts at Union Theological Seminary. He is focusing his studies on Black Liberation Theology.

I wake up at 6:30 in the morning in my room in Old Jerusalem and turn on the BBC. I see that the United Nations fact-finding mission has been denied entry into the refugee camp of Jenin for at least a few more days. What's a few more days after being denied entry for several weeks?

After several hours on a bus, the driver lets us out on a pathway that would take us from Israel to Palestine. The International Solidarity Movement (ISM) had successfully used this path a few weeks ago. The main roadways are blocked by military checkpoints which are not letting anyone in. This pathway now has a military checkpoint and these soldiers also refuse to let us through. They ask Huwaida, the only Palestinian in our group for her papers and then they spot me—the only African-American in the group—and ask for mine. The rest of the group, who are Europeans and European Americans, they don't see fit to harass. We then all turn around and look for another way into Palestine.

Lucky for us our bus driver waited to see if we would make it across. After conversations between our driver and local Palestinians we are driven to another pathway into Palestine. There is an Israeli military patrol blocking this pathway. After ten minutes it moves to patrol another area. Our group then jumps out of the bus and makes its way across the border.

We hurriedly walk through some woods and up a little hill where some vans are waiting for anyone who gets through the border. The vans then take us on to Jenin.

By about 2:30 we enter the outskirts of Jenin. Though this is supposed to be one of the bloodiest scenes of the most recent Israeli invasion into Palestine, at first there is little sign of the invasion. As we pull into town, I see what was a police station now in rubble. I see smashed cars that have been run over by tanks, light poles that have also been run down. People are in the streets sweeping up the dust that is all over the ground and in the air from the invasion. Windows have been shot out and there are bullet holes along the walls but the buildings themselves are still standing.

We make our way to a volunteer medical headquarters staffed by Palestinians. They greet us with the celebrated hospitality of the Palestinians and serve us all tea. They explain to us that Jenin is a refugee camp that has turned into a city of fourteen thousand. The residents of Jenin are the results of the ethnic cleansing required to establish a new state with a foreign people. The push by European Jewry to create the state of Israel created 800,000 refugees, who over fifty years later have grown to a near 6 million Palestinians scattered throughout the world. Palestinian refugees who are outside of Israel and Palestine are never allowed to return, though each year thousands of Jews from Russia, Ethiopia, and elsewhere are guaranteed their "right to return."

After a little more than an hour at the hospital we finally enter central Jenin. For a square kilometer there is nothing but homes and apartment buildings lying in rubble. Cars are crushed, homes bombed. It is hard to imagine that this destruction was brought by a human force. It looks like a massive earthquake hit the area, except there are bullet holes piercing the walls that are still standing. As I made my way through the rubble I heard occasional explosions. I had heard that there were still ordinances (tank shells, explosives, etc.) that had not blown up and were still liable to explode. A couple days ago, a ten-year-old set off one of these ordinances and was killed.

One of the most disturbing aspects of witnessing this aftermath is the complete invisibility of humanitarian aid. There were two bulldozers in the entire town both manned by Palestinians. I thought that when an area has been hit by a terrible disaster the world sends in their search and rescue teams, emergency shelters are created for the people who have lost their homes, and construction crews are sent in to help rebuild. For the Palestinians the world simply waits until Israel allows their journalists to come in and take pictures of the destruction. The mass humanitarian aid sent to other parts of the world simply does not arrive for the Palestinians.

In one of the buildings located on the outskirts of the center of the destroyed area there is some graffiti was written in English. Hip hop is very popular among the Palestinian youth because they relate well to the hopelessness, the anger, and the rage that is so well-articulated in the music of hip hop. Scrawled on the wall of this building standing on the edge of the mass destruction was "We Will Stay Here" and the phrase I think Biggie Smalls popularized, "Born to Die." It actually said "Born to Dead," but I know what they meant.

After slipping back into Israel and again having the Israeli military ask solely for the identification papers of the only Palestinian-American and myself the only African-American, I find myself in my bed in East Jerusalem watching the eleven PM BBC news. Colin Powell is on television saying that he knows of no evidence of a massacre or mass graves in Jenin. I don't know what the definition of massacre is but at least 40 bodies have been found in Jenin, and most of the rubble has not yet been cleared. I am sure Colin Powell does not have any evidence of a massacre or mass graves or much of anything else. He has never been to Jenin and the UN fact-finding mission still has not been allowed to enter Jenin.

What *did* happen in Jenin and throughout what was considered Palestine will go down in history as crimes against humanity. One of the strongest military forces in the world stormed what were in effect housing projects, and destroyed property and life at whim. Then they refused medical treatment to the wounded for days, sometimes for weeks. They prevented journalists or independent investigative teams to go into these areas and document what occurred. Israel invaded Palestine and Jenin, in particular, to stop suicide bombers from attacking Israel. Does anyone truly think that rampant destruction, mass arrest, and mass executions are going to weaken the will of Palestinians to kill Israelis? I learned in the US that if there is no justice there will be no peace. We must bring justice to the Palestinian people. That is the only way to have peace in the Middle East.

change@yahoo.com

John Caruso

*John Caruso is a Silicon Valley technical consultant. He traveled to
Jenin as a participant with the International Solidarity Movement.
Caruso was also involved in the action at Palestinian President
Yasser Arafat's compound, when several internationals entered
his compound while it was besieged by the Israeli army. He was a
part of the action of entering the Church of the Nativity, which was
under Israeli siege as well.*

I entered Jenin as part of a group of international activists on April 22,
2002. As we drove into the camp, the evidence of the Israeli invasion was
immediately apparent—utility and phone lines had been cut just outside
the camp. On the walls and on the doors of houses, about every 10 or
15 feet, the Star of David had been spray-painted in black paint. Some
of the stars had exclamation points or "#1!" written inside of them. The
message of humiliation and control was clear; Israeli troops here had
been marking their territory, making a racial and religious statement to
every person in the town. Thoughts of Kristallnacht came unbidden to
my mind, and the irony was palpable.

As we walked toward the center of the camp, we passed house after
house that had been partially or completely demolished. I was standing
next to one house, a third of which had simply been shaved off and
was lying there on the ground in an unidentifiable tangle of rubble. The
closest room was the living room, and I could see the hardwood floor
inside abruptly ending where a tank or bulldozer had taken it out. I
wondered what had happened to the family that lived there.

In the center of the camp, an area comprising several city blocks
had been completely razed by Israeli bulldozers and tanks. We walked
up onto a rubble pile. It was so wide and high that it had a terrain of
its own and in places was as tall as a three-story house. You could see
people's personal belongings crushed and twisted underneath the stone.
The wheels of a mangled baby carriage pointed toward the sky at the
top of one rise. As I walked on this horrifying monument to brutality, I
realized that I was standing on a tomb. Some people had not been able
to escape their houses before the bulldozers came, and they had been
buried alive—trapped inside as the walls collapsed in on them.

There were still unexploded munitions in the rubble pile, and at least one or two people each day were being killed or losing arms or legs as they dug through the wreckage. Despite the dangers, they were determined to find their loved ones, their houses, or their belongings—and who could blame them? Their lives had been destroyed, buried under tons of stone, and they were doing whatever they could to get them back.

A Palestinian man motioned us into a Jenin mosque, and I was appalled by what I saw when I went inside. There were stains all over the carpet—food, blood, dirt, and other things I couldn't identify. Prayer mats were crumpled all around. There were cans of food (with Hebrew writing) and bottles thrown on every part of the floor. There were empty spray paint cans—no doubt the source of some of the Stars of David I had seen around the camp. The collection boxes had been overturned and the bottoms broken through, and the money was missing from them. There were books strewn about, including copies of the Quran, some with pages ripped out.

On the roof of the mosque I saw that the Israelis had chosen this location because it was the high ground in town, provided a panoramic view of the camp, and was the perfect location for the Israeli snipers. Near the door to the roof, a stereo speaker had been broken through and used as a toilet by the Israeli soldiers. As with most buildings in Jenin, there were large water tanks on top of the mosque, and the Israelis had riddled them with dozens of bullet holes. Attacking water resources is a textbook war crime, but this had not stopped the Israeli military from doing it throughout the West Bank during its assault.

The worst was yet to come. In the lowest level of the mosque there was a school for kids—a kindergarten probably, inferred from construction paper mobiles hanging from the ceiling and the colorful drawings all around. But this fact had not spared it the same treatment the Israelis had visited on the rest of the mosque. Desks were lying toppled on the floor, and papers had been thrown everywhere. The two classrooms I saw had been completely torn up. One of them was difficult to enter because of the stench—the Israeli soldiers had used a small basket and a box next to it as a toilet, and the smell filled the room. There was a bathroom not 25 paces from this room, but instead of using it they had opted to leave their "mark" here, just as they had on the roof. Children's drawings of robots and animals covered the floor, torn off the walls or from shelves. On the blackboard one of the soldiers had drawn a Star of David in chalk—here,

225

in a children's classroom.

But the most shocking of all was what they had done to a series of large paintings on the concrete wall of the basement. The paintings drawn on the concrete showed a little girl in a red dress doing everyday things: talking to her mother, sitting in a field, playing with a boat in the bathtub. An Israeli soldier or soldiers had gone through and cut the eyes out of each of the paintings—and not haphazardly, but very carefully, following the exact outline of the eyes. Five paintings; five sets of eyes missing. I thought about how much time it must have taken to do this, especially since the paintings were done directly on the concrete. Someone had spent a long time here with a knife, working carefully and methodically. I saw many things in my two weeks in the West Bank, but none of them chilled me as much as this sickening tableau.

The Israeli government has waged a relentless propaganda campaign to counter the damage caused to its reputation by its actions in Jenin. But having seen it with my own eyes, there is no doubt in my mind: This was terrorism.

caruso@paradiso.umuc.edu

Terje Roed-Larsen

Terje Roed-Larsen is the UN Special Coordinator in the Occupied Territories of the United Nations envoy to the Middle East.

I think I can speak for all in the UN delegation (in saying) that we are shocked. Just seeing this area, it looks like there's been an earthquake here, and the stench of death is strong in many places where we are standing.

I think this is absolutely, totally unacceptable and unheard of that an occupying power keeps a curfew and keeps a huge proportion of the civilian population suffering day by day. This has to stop. . . . the smell was horrible—decaying corpses below the rubble. And we saw, for instance, a twelve-year-old boy being—with some people digging with their hands—they were digging him out, and his burned completely, demolished body. We saw, for instance, two brothers who were digging out their father and their other brothers below the rubble, the corpses were in pieces. It was horrible, an absolutely unbelievable scene.

And what we also know after our visit is that there must be about 2,000 people who do not have roofs above their heads. They need shelter immediately. We also know that there is an acute need of food, water, and medicine. The electricity system is completely destroyed. The water pipes are cut. It is a scene of a catastrophe of major proportions. It looks as if there has been an earthquake there.

Excerpts taken from "UN Envoy: Jenin is 'Horrifying Beyond Belief'" in *Ha'aretz Daily,* and *CNN.com* "'Horrifying' scene at Jenin, UN envoy says" April 18, 2002.

Norman G. Finkelstein

Norman G. Finkelstein received his doctorate from the Department of Politics, Princeton University, for a thesis on the theory of Zionism. He is the author of four books: Image and Reality of the Israel-Palestine Conflict *(Verso, 1995),* The Rise and Fall of Palestine *(University of Minnesota, 1996); with Ruth Bettina Birn,* A Nation on Trial: The Goldhagen Thesis and Historical Truth *(Henry Holt, 1998) and* The Holocaust Industry: Reflections on the Exploitation of Jewish Suffering *(Verso, 2000). His writings have appeared in prestigious journals such as the* London Review of Books, Index on Censorship, Journal of Palestine Studies, New Left Review, Middle East Report, Christian Science Monitor *and* Al-Ahram Weekly. *Currently he teaches political science at DePaul University in Chicago.*

The Western media is replete with stories about what Jenin was not: it wasn't a massacre; several hundred Palestinians weren't killed; there weren't mass graves; etc., etc. What's missing in all this news "coverage" is the truth about what exactly did happen in Jenin. None are better equipped to tell us than the survivors themselves. Without their testimonies, Jenin would have become just one more unmarked grave in the sorrowful history of Palestine's conquest. Like other readers, I am grateful to the editors of this volume for preserving the truth of Jenin's martyrdom for future generations—and, in doing so, redeeming in some small measure the suffering endured there.

NormanGF@hotmail.com

Dr. Alfred M. Lilienthal

Lilienthal is a graduate of Cornell University and Columbia Law School. He later served with the Department of State and as a consultant to the American delegation at the organizing meeting of the United Nations in San Francisco. He has traveled over 25 times to the Middle East for firsthand investigation of events and authored several books including The Zionist Connection.

We know from past experience what the Israeli reaction will be to being confronted with the truth about Jenin. I clearly recall that when I visited Deir Yassin many years ago, the pervasive Israeli belief was that there was no such thing as a Deir Yassin massacre. It was a myth, they said. But Deir Yassin was unfortunately a grim reality in which so many Palestinian lives were expunged in 1948.

Cover-ups and war crimes by other nations have been exposed, but never as effectively as is needed against the Israelis. Milosovic and Sharon—two of the world's worst war criminals, who have been literally getting away with murder—both have to be held fully accountable under international law. Milosovic is on trial as he should be, and Sharon also belongs before a court of justice. His crimes must be fully exposed. I remember how outraged I was at the time, when I went to get the facts at Qibya, where Sharon's special killer Unit 101 had massacred Palestinian villagers in 1953. Later I went to the Sabra and Shatila refugee camps in Lebanon where so many innocent women and children were slaughtered in 1982 due to Sharon's duplicity. I visited there with tears in my eyes.

What Israelis and Zionists have savagely done to the Palestinians for over fifty years has never been explained to the American public. Until we address the well-documented present realities, we can make no meaningful progress toward a two-state solution with peace and safety for both the Palestinians and the Israelis.

AlfredLilienthal@aol.com

Mazin B. Qumsiyeh, PhD

Dr. Qumsiyeh is an associate Professor at Yale University School of Medicine and co-founder and spokesperson of the Palestine Right to Return Coalition.

We all learned with horror about the unfolding tragedy as Israeli occupation forces attacked the Jenin refugee camp and left, in its wake, one quarter of the camp residents' homes destroyed. But for me personally, the dominant thought was the unfairness of this atrocity occurring to people who are living in a destitute refugee camp. According to UNWRA, the UN group in charge of providing humanitarian aid to Palestinian refugees: "Most of the camp's residents came from villages which can be seen from the camp and, which today, lie inside the Green Line in Israel. Many of the refugees still maintain close ties with their relatives in those villages."

There are over 13,000 refugees in the Jenin camp cramped on 373 *dunums* (about 93 acres). They are the villagers and their progeny who fled their lands in 1948 and were prevented from returning. Their confiscated lands total over 110,000 *dunums*. Villagers were forced to permanently flee places with names like Ain Al-Mansi ("spring of the forgotten"), and Khirbet Al-Jawfa, Al-Lajjun (ancient Megiddo), and Al-Mazar. Very few of the buildings in these ancient and idyllic villages remain. At Al-Lajjun, one of the few remaining buildings is the village mosque which is now used as a carpentry shop by the Jewish settlement of Kibbutz Megiddo. It is criminal for these native villagers to be uprooted, disinherited, and prevented from returning to their lands to lead a normal life.

For them to be subjected to repeated atrocities, while they survive in the tiny ghetto known as Jenin Refugee Camp, is beyond human comprehension. Justice demands these refugees be allowed to return to their lands and to bury their dead in their ancient villages. There can simply be no peace or security without justice.

mbq2@email.med.yale.edu

Robert Jensen

Robert Jensen is a professor of journalism at the University of Texas at Austin, a member of the Nowar Collective, and author of the book Writing Dissent: Taking Radical Ideas from the Margins to the Mainstream.

The moral level of the powerful reaches a new low when there are serious discussions about whether an obviously illegal assault on a civilian population is a full-fledged massacre or just a routine war crime. But that has been the nature of the debate of the Israeli attack on Jenin. In the United States it is even worse.

Some Americans rationalize Israeli brutality as necessary in the war on terrorism. Others are willing to condemn Israel's worst offenses. But too few are willing to take the next step and realize that Israeli brutality is American brutality. Israeli aggression and the illegal occupation of Palestinian land can happen only because the US government allows it to happen. If not for US financial and military aid, along with political and diplomatic support, Israel could not continue these operations or the occupation.

That means that in moral terms, US citizens have an obligation to organize and speak out to end this madness. We must demand peace, but peace that brings justice to Palestine. Palestine is half a world away from the United States, but Palestine is a moral test for US citizens. So far, we have failed. For the sake of Palestine and Israel—and the United States—I hope we can find that moral strength.

rjensen@uts.cc.utexas.edu

Arjan al-Fassed

Mr. al-Fassed is a Palestinian human rights activist living in the Occupied Palestinian Territories and is affiliated with LAW—The Palestinian Society for the Protection of Human Rights.

When people read the news and hear about atrocities committed by Israeli soldiers, most move their eyebrows and carry on. It's Israel after all—they're the exception, the victim, the impossible aggressor, even though statistics, documents, United Nations reports, and other witnesses indicate something very different. Is the world waiting for another Sabra and Shatila? Another Sebrenica? Bosnia or Kosovo? Rwanda, East Timor? New York or Kandahar?

Just tell me how many need to get killed, before I start pressing my demands again. Just tell me how many homes must be demolished, before I can stop counting and demand compensation? Just tell me the number of war crimes at which I can lay my pen to rest and demand the world end Israeli impunity. For the time being, I'm sick and tired.

www.arjanalawsociety.org

Francis A. Boyle

Professor Boyle is a human rights lawyer and professor of law at the University of Illinois. He is the author of The Criminality of Nuclear Deterrence, *recently published by Clarity Press. His other books include* Defending Civil Resistance Under International Law, The Future of International Law and American Foreign Policy, World Politics and International Law, *as well as major articles on a range of international law and human rights issues.*

The Israeli government inflicted war crimes, grave breaches of the Fourth Geneva Convention of 1949, and a crime against humanity upon the inhabitants of Jenin. The United Nations must prosecute these international crimes for the exact same reasons that it created the International Criminal Tribunal for the former Yugoslavia and the International Criminal Tribunal for Rwanda. Both of these ad hoc international criminal tribunals were established by the United Nations Security Council with the approval of the United States government, a permanent member with veto power.

It has already been publicly reported, however, that the Bush Jr. administration intervened with UN Secretary General Kofi Annan to head off an investigation of Jenin as authorized by UN Security Council Resolution 1405 (April 19, 2002). Despite such unconscionable but continual US obstructionism at the Security Council, the UN nevertheless holds responsibility for protecting the basic human rights of the Palestinian people. The UN General Assembly has concurrent jurisdiction under the United Nations Charter to investigate and prosecute Israeli government officials—both civilian and military—for the international crimes that they have ordered, committed, condoned, and approved at Jenin and elsewhere in Palestine.

We must pressure the member states of the UN General Assembly to establish an International Criminal Tribunal for Palestine (ICTP) in order to prosecute Israeli war criminals, both military and civilian, including, and especially, Israeli political leaders such as Sharon. The UN General Assembly can set up this ICTP by a majority vote pursuant to its powers to establish "subsidiary organs" under UN Charter Article 22. This International Criminal Tribunal for Palestine should be organized by the UN General Assembly along the same lines as the International Criminal Tribunal for the Former Yugoslavia, which deals with international armed conflicts.

In this regard, back in 1993 as the Lawyer for the Republic of Bosnia and Herzegovina, I sued the rump of Yugoslavia for committing genocide, crimes against humanity, war crimes, and grave breaches of the Fourth Geneva Convention before the International Court of Justice in The Hague. I also did the very best I could to personally implicate Slobodan Milosevic and his henchmen for ordering and committing these international crimes against the Bosnians. At the time I never realistically expected that less than nine years later Milosevic himself and his henchmen would be on trial in The Hague for committing these heinous international crimes against the Bosnians.

For similar reasons, Sharon and his henchmen must also stand trial in The Hague for perpetrating the exact same types of international crimes against the Palestinian people at Jenin and elsewhere in Palestine. It is up to us to bring Sharon and his henchmen to justice in The Hague. Milosevic and Sharon will get along quite well with each other in The Hague because they have so much in common to talk about: war crimes, crimes against humanity, and genocide.

fboyle@law.uiuc.edu

Sam Bahour

Mr. Bahour is a Palestinian-American writer living in the Palestinian city of Al-Bireh in the West Bank. He is co-author of Homeland: Oral Histories of Palestine and Palestinians *(1994).*

I sat in Al-Bireh/Ramallah with my wife, Abeer, and two daughters, Areen, 8, and Nadine, 2, under strict military curfew as we witnessed the Israeli military heyday in Jenin. We watched and listened to the news reports in shock and anger as explosions thundered and Israeli tanks rumbled all around our home. Huddled around the television between the electrical outages to witness this atrocity unravel, my only thought was that this dose of colonist shock by Israel was different than those of 1948 and 1967. This time no one fled, no one moved, no one panicked. We only wept with anger and internalized a vow that Jenin would never be forgotten.

Today, Jenin, the city and the refugee camp, is embodied in every Palestinian. Jenin, the latest collective memory milestone in our struggle to end Israeli occupation joins the ranks of Deir Yassin, Kufr Kassem, Qibya, Emmwas, Yalo, Sabra and Shatila. This time the world watched Jenin scream for help and was silent. Even after the Israeli tanks, bulldozers, helicopters, armored personnel carriers and soldiers finally pulled back, the world remained silent. Rest assured that the children of Jenin, those who made it out of the rubble of their homes will never forget. Never remain silent. How can they while Jenin continues screaming for help?

sbahour@palnet.com

Peter Hansen

Peter Hansen heads the United Nations Relief and Works Agency, UNRWA.

We are getting reports of pure horror—that helicopters are strafing residential areas, that systematic shelling by tanks has created hundreds of wounded, that bulldozers are razing refugee homes and that food and medicine will soon run out. In the name of human decency the Israeli military must allow our ambulances safe passage to help evacuate the wounded and deliver emergency supplies of medicine and food.

I had hoped that the horror stories of Jenin were exaggerated and influenced by the emotions engaged but I am afraid these were not exaggerated and that Jenin camp residents lived through a human catastrophe that have few parallels in recent history."

Excerpts taken from "Israel digs mass graves—covering up war crimes" LAW Press Release April 10, 2002 and UNRWA Press Release April 18, 2002.

Prof. Derrick Pounder

Professor Pounder is a forensic medicine expert from University of Dundee (UK) and part of an Amnesty International team granted access to Jenin.

Claims that a large number of civilians died and are under the rubble are highly credible. It is not believable that only a few people have been killed, given the reports we have that a large number of people were inside three and four-story buildings when they were demolished.

The autopsy of a thirty-eight-year-old Palestinian revealed that he was either shot in the foot, and then in the back, or shot in the back first—receiving a fatal wound—and his corpse was for some reason shot in the foot. Whichever order the shots occurred in, it was highly suspicious.

Interview with Prof. Pounder in "Fresh evidence of Jenin atrocities" by Phil Reeves, *The Independent (UK),* April 18, 2002.

Javier Zuniga

Mr. Zuniga is an Amnesty International delegate.

This is one of the worst scenes of devastation I have ever witnessed. It is almost impossible to conceive that what was once a town is now this lunar landscape. There is a real possibility that people are still alive under the rubble of their former homes; one of our colleagues from a local human rights organization received a phone call from a family of 10 who were trapped below ground and asking for help, yet there is no evidence of concerted efforts to search for and rescue survivors.

"Jenin Refugee Camp: Amnesty International Calls for Immediate International Humanitarian Assistance" Amnesty International Press Release April 17, 2002.

Rene Kosirnik

Rene Kosirnik heads the regional delegation of the International Committee of the Red Cross (ICRC).

The truth will come out, as it has come out in Bosnia and Kosovo, as it has in other places where we've had these kinds of allegations. I must say that the evidence before us at the moment doesn't lead us to believe that the allegations are anything other than truthful and that, therefore, there are large numbers of civilians dead underneath these bulldozed and bombed ruins that we see.

We know there are families who were there and killed and buried. We were on the ruins yesterday and two elderly men came forward, each of them pointed to where their houses had been. And one of them told us that 10 members of his family were buried under the rubble.

"Jenin Massacre Evidence Growing" BBC News April 18, 2002.

Confirmed Palestinian Deaths

Fadwa Fathi al-Jamal, 27, female
  Civilian.
  She was shot in the waist and abdomen by an Israeli sniper.

Ziad Ibrahim Amr, 37, male
  Fighter in Al-Aqsa Brigades.
  He died from a gunshot wound to the head fired by an Israeli sniper.

Hani Ateiah Abu Irmilat, 19, male
  Civilian.
  He was shot in the chest and abdomen by Israeli snipers.

Ali Khaled Masharqa, 19, male
  Fighter in Al-Aqsa Brigades.
  While attempting to rescue a wounded civilian, he was shot by an Israeli sniper.

Muhammad Omar Hawashin, 13, male
  Civilian.
  He was killed by an Israeli sniper.

Rabee Ahmed Jalamneh, 21, male
  Fighter in Al-Aqsa Brigade.
  He was shot in the head and chest by Israeli snipers.

Ali Na'el Mqasqas, 15, male
  Civilian.
  He was killed at home by an Israeli sniper who shot him in the head.

Nidal Muhammad Swetat, 20, male
Fighter in Hamas.
He was shot by Israeli forces while attempting to rescue two wounded police officers.

Muhammad Masoud Abu al-Sibah, 65, male
Civilian.
He was crushed to death when Israelis demolished his home while he was inside. His body was not recovered until eighteen days after the invasion ended.

Jamal Essa Sabbagh, 35, male
Civilian.
He was executed by Israeli forces and his body was crushed by tanks.

Nizar Saed Matahin, 24, male
Fighter in Hamas.
He was hit and killed by aircraft fire while trying to rescue a wounded officer of the Palestinian Authority.

Ahmed Bashir Hamduni, 72, male
Civilian.
He was shot and wounded while fleeing his burning house, after which he was taken and executed with a shot to the head.

Mariam Abdullah Wishahe, 52, female
Civilian.
She was shot in the head and chest by an Israeli sniper.

Yusrah Muhammad Abu Khorj, 60, female
Civilian.
She was a mentally disabled woman who died when an Israeli missile hit her. Yusrah's body was completely dismembered.

Waddah Fathi al-Shalabi, 38, male
Civilian.
He and his neighbor were executed with shots to the head.

Abdelkarim al-Sadi, 21, male
Civilian.
He and his neighbor were executed by shots to the head.

Taha Muhammad Z'byde, 24, male
Fighter in Islamic Jihad.
He was shot in the neck by an Israeli sniper. Later, his body was
burned and could only be identified by his wristwatch.

Mustafa Abdelrahim al-Shalabi, 38, male
Fighter in Hamas.
He was killed when his house was shelled.

Ashraf Mahmud Abu al-Hayjah, 23, male
Fighter in Hamas.
He was shot in the head while attempting to rescue a civilian, after
which his body was burned.

Alam Abed Sayas, 26, male
Fighter, unknown faction.
He was shot in the chest by an Israeli sniper.

Muhammad Khalil Masharkah, 33, male
Fighter in Hamas.
He was shot in the arm, head, and chest by fire from an Israeli airplane.

Ameed Azme Abu al-Hassan, 17, male
Civilian.
He was shot in the neck by Israeli forces in a helicopter.

Amjad Hussein al-Fayed, 30, male
Fighter in Hamas.
He was killed by Israeli forces firing from a helicopter.

Muhammad Hussein al-Fayed, 19, male
Fighter in Hamas.
He was shot in the chest and his house was demolished, crushing his
body.

Shadi Muhammad Nubani, 19, male
    Fighter in Islamic Jihad.
    His body was crushed when a house was demolished.

Abdelrahim Ahmed Faraj, 25, male
    Fighter in Islamic Jihad.
    He was killed in clashes with Israeli forces.

Nidal Muhammad Ighbarieh, 35, male
    Police officer with the Palestinian Authority.
    He was shot by an Israeli sniper then his body was crushed during a
    house demolition.

Muhammad Khalil Nawrasi, 34, male
    Security Officer with Palestinian Authority.
    He was shot in the chest and face in clashes with Israeli forces.

Muhammad Mahmud Taleb, 20, male
    Fighter, unknown faction.
    He was killed along with other fighters when the house they were in
    was shelled.

Abdel Nasser Mahmud Hatub, 38, male
    Civilian.
    First he was shot and wounded. Later Israeli forces entered his house
    and fatally shot him.

Ali Mahmud Khamayseh, 72, male
    Civilian.
    He died from an asthma attack triggered by tear gas shot into his
    home. Snipers prevented neighbors from coming to his aid.

Attieh Hassan Irmilat, 44, male
    Civilian.
    He was shot by a sniper in the head while in his home.

Ifaf Ali Dusuki, 54, female
    Civilian.

She was killed when Israelis blew her front door open with explosives.

Zuhair Majdi Istiti, 30, male
Fighter in Al-Aqsa Brigades.
He was shot in clashes with Israelis and died three days later from his wounds.

Na'ef Kassem al-Na'ef, 19, male
Civilian.
He was killed by an Israeli airplane ordnance.

Jamal Tawfiq Ararawi, 33, male
Civilian.
He was executed in front of his wife and children.

Kamal Saed al-Saghir, 55, male
Civilian.
He was a mentally disabled man who was run over and crushed by an Israeli tank.

Jaber Hosni Jabber, 21, male
Civilian.
He was shot by Israeli forces in the feet and the head. His body was crushed when the house he died in was demolished. It was not recovered until 20 days after the invasion.

Riyad Muhammad B'der, 56, male
Fighter, unknown faction.
He was a resident of Tulkarm, who came to Jenin the day before the invasion started in order to defend the camp. He was killed while fighting against Israeli forces.

Munther Amin al-Haj, 21, male
Police Officer with the Palestinian Authority.
He was first shot and wounded by Israeli forces. Then, as he was being helped to the hospital for treatment, an Israeli sniper fatally shot him.

Faris Emad Zubin, 13, male
Civilian.
He was killed by a gunshot wound to the heart fired by Israeli forces.

Tariq Ziad Darwish, 25, male
Civilian.
He was shot in the head by Israeli forces.

Fadi Kamal Kassem, 19, male
Affiliation unknown.
The circumstances of his death are unknown.

Waleed Ibrahim Mahmud, 25, male
Affiliation unknown.
He was shot in the head and abdomen by Israeli forces.

Yusuf Ahmed Kabha (Abu Jandal), 35, male
Officer in the Palestinian Authority.
He was shot in the head, neck, and abdomen in an Israeli execution.

Majdi Naji Khleleh, 15, male
Civilian.
Israeli forces shot him in the abdomen.

Nidal Hosni Abu al-Hayjah, 23, male
Affiliation unknown.
Israeli forces shot him a total of twelve times in the head and abdomen.

Mahmud Mousa Tawalbe, 24, male
Fighter in Islamic Jihad.
An Israeli missile struck and killed him.

Mahmud Abu Hilweh, 24, male
Fighter in Hamas.
He was killed by the Israeli army in the Hawashin neighborhood.

Qais Udwan, age unknown, male
   Fighter in Hamas.
   He was killed by Israeli aircraft.

Saed Awad, age unknown, male
   Affiliation unknown.
   He was killed by an Israeli airplane raid.

Majdi Balasmih, age unknown, male
   Affiliation unknown.
   He was killed by an Israeli airplane raid.

Munketh Swafta, age unknown, male
   Affiliation unknown.
   He was killed by an Israeli airplane raid.

Ashraf Daragmeh, age unknown, male
   Affiliation unknown.
   The circumstances of his death are unknown.

Muhammad Kamil, age unknown, male
   Affiliation unknown.
   The circumstances of his death are unknown.

Hosni Ali Amer, 45, male
   Civilian.
   He was arrested by the Israelis and later died in their custody. His
   family claims that he died from torture at the hands of the Israelis.

Mahmud Muhammad Abu Jildeh, 70, male
   Civilian.
   Israeli forces shot him multiple times.

Assad Faisal Qurani, 10, male
   Civilian.
   Assad was killed by an exploding shell fired from a tank.

Muneer Essa Wishahe, 18, male
Civilian.
An Israeli sniper shot him in the back, and his body was crushed in a house demolition.

Murad Abdelhakim al-Ghul, 16, male
Civilian.
He was killed when tank ordnance exploded near him.

Unidentified body A, age unknown
Affiliation unknown.
The body was recovered from under the rubble and was unable to be identified.

Unidentified body B, age unknown
Affiliation unknown.
The body was recovered from under the rubble in the Hawashin neighborhood, and could not be identified.

Unidentified infant body, age unknown
Civilian.
The body was recovered from under the rubble and was unable to be identified.

In the April 2002 invasion approximately 250 people were wounded. There are approximately 300 Jenin residents in Israeli prisons at the time this book goes to print.

Photographs of Jenin

258

Glossary

Abu

Meaning "father of," this prefix is used in the Arab and Muslim world at the beginning a man's name, followed most often by the name of his firstborn son, e.g. Abu Muhammad, or "the father of Muhammad."

Abu Jandal

Also known as Yusuf Ahmed Kabha, Abu Jandal was from the village of Yabad, located in the West Bank. He was a member of the Fatah movement in exile. He later returned along with many others after the signing of the Oslo Accords to Palestine. Abu Jandal, although not a resident of Jenin, was known as one of the main leaders of the resistance against Israeli forces.

Abu Jihad

Also known as Khalil Ibrahim Al-Wazir, Abu Jihad was born October 10, 1935 in the town of Ramla, Palestine. Abu Jihad was believed to be the military strategist and second in command of the Palestine Liberation Organization (PLO).

Abu Sibah neighborhood.

For location see map.

Al-Aqsa Brigades

A military off-shoot of the Fatah movement. It is the largest faction of the PLO and was established during the 2000 Al-Aqsa Intifada as a response to the Israeli military occupation.

Al-Qassam Brigades

The military wing of the Islamic Movement, Hamas, founded in the Nuseirat refugee camp in Gaza in the late 1980s, to later become one of the strongest Palestinian military movements in the occupied territories.

APC

Armored personnel carrier.

Ashkelon Prison

Ashkelon Prison is located in southern Israel within pre-1967 Israel. It is a major detention center for Palestinians from the Occupied Territories of the West Bank and Gaza.

B'Tselem

The Israeli Center for Human Rights in the Occupied Territories. B'Tselem was established in 1989 by a group of academics, attorneys, journalists, and Knesset members. It "endeavors to document and educate the Israeli public and policy makers about human rights violations in the Occupied Territories, combat the phenomenon of denial prevalent among the Israeli public, and help create a human rights culture in Israel."

Dammaj neighborhood

For location see map.

Dr. Khalil Sulieman

The Head of the Palestinian Red Crescent Society Emergency Medical Service (EMS) in Jenin, Dr. Khalil Sulieman, 58, was killed on March 4, 2002 while he was evacuating an injured girl in a PRCS ambulance from the Jenin refugee camp. He was shot and killed by Israeli tank fire as he tried to enter the Jenin camp in his ambulance. Witnesses say that he was alive for an hour and a half after having been shot. Because of the Israeli siege around the camp, he did not receive any medical attention.

Dunum

A unit of land equaling approximately one quarter acre.

Fatah

The largest Palestinian faction of the PLO, founded in the late 1960s by the current Palestinian Authority President, Yasser Arafat. The movement is largely political but it has several military offshoots, most prominently, the Al-Aqsa Brigades.

Hamas

Also known as the Islamic Resistance Movement, Hamas was founded in the late 1980s a few months after the first Palestinian Intifada against the Israeli military occupation. As well as their military actions to end the Israeli occupation, Hamas is also engaged in development programs, such as running hospitals and schools in the occupied territories. The movement is regarded by Israel and the United States as a terrorist organization.

Harsch Al-Sa'ada

An agricultural area on the outskirts of Jenin refugee camp that was used as a point of assembly by Israeli forces. Witnesses claim that many residents of the camp were also gathered and tortured here before they were transferred to other detention centers.

Hijab

A scarf worn by women throughout the Arab and Muslim world.

Imam

A religious cleric in the Islamic faith. The man who leads prayers in mosques and delivers sermons.

International Criminal Tribunal in the Hague

The Geneva Conventions established the principles used to determine cases of genocide. These were later applied to the war crimes trials in Nuremberg and Tokyo after the Second World War. In 1993 the United Nations Security Council established the International Criminal Tribunal for the former Yugoslavia (ICTY) in The Hague. This was followed in 1994 by the International Criminal Tribunal for Rwanda (ICTR) in Arusha, Tanzania. These two courts have clarified the Geneva Conventions and reasserted the international community's determination to eliminate the crime of genocide. In 2002 The Rome Convention came into effect. A permanent International Criminal Court is now being established in The Hague to try cases of genocide, war crimes, and crimes against humanity. The ICC will refer to the Geneva Conventions and build upon precedents set by the international courts preceding it.

Islamic Jihad Movement

Originating in the Gaza Strip in the 1970s, the Islamic Jihad movement was created to oppose the Israeli military occupation. It is one of the smaller factions and has a much smaller support base than the Islamic movement Hamas.

Jabriat neighborhood

Also know as "Jawabra" neighborhood. For location see map.

Jurit Al-Dahab neighborhood

For location see map.

Kristallnacht

Or The Night of Broken Glass. A massive, coordinated attack on Jews throughout the German Reich on the night of November 9, 1938.

Kaffiah

A headdress worn by Palestinian men, as well as men throughout the Arab world. Although it is traditionally worn by men, women also wear the Kaffiah. It is an expression of nationalism and solidarity with the Palestinian struggle.

Mahmud Tawalbe

The residents of Jenin's refugee camp recognize Mahmud Tawalbe as a leader of the resistance. Many say that he directed the resistance in Jenin. He belonged to Islamic Jihad.

Masjid Abdullah Azzam neighborhood

A neighborhood located on the west side of Jenin refugee camp.

Megiddo Prison

A military prison in the lower Galilee within Israel that was established during the first Palestinian uprising. It is mainly used for the incarceration of political prisoners.

Ofra Prison

An Israeli prison constructed near the West Bank city of Ramallah in an Israeli military camp located in the Ofra Jewish settlement. It was first used to host the Jenin prisoners. The prison is known among Palestinians for its harsh conditions and brutal treatment of prisoners.

Prima facie

A legal term meaning true, valid, or adequate at first sight; as it seems at first sight; ostensible; self-evident; obvious. In law it is sufficient to establish a fact or a case unless disproved.

Palestine Red Crescent Society (PRCS)

Established in 1968, PRCS is a national humanitarian society that provides a wide range of health, social, and other humanitarian services for the Palestinian people throughout the Middle East.

Rumana village

A village located near Jenin. For location see map.

Sahah

The center square of the Jenin refugee camp. For location see map.

Sahl Ibn Amr

Flat land north of the camp.

Salem

The headquarters for the Israeli intelligence and military administration. This is often where Palestinians are taken to be interrogated.

Saraya al-Quds

The military wing of the Islamic Jihad Movement.

Shebab

Literally meaning "youth." The term *shebab* is also used to refer to the young fighters who defended the Jenin refugee camp.

Um

Meaning "mother of," this prefix is used in the Arab and Muslim world at the beginning of a woman's name, followed most often by the name of her firstborn son, e.g. Um Muhammad, or "the mother of Muhammad."

UNICEF

Created by the United Nations General Assembly in 1946 to help children after World War II in Europe, UNICEF was first known as the United Nations International Children's Emergency Fund. In 1953, UNICEF became a permanent part of the United Nations system, its task being to help children living in poverty in developing countries. Its name was shortened to the United Nations Children's Fund, but it continues to use the acronym "UNICEF."

UNRWA

The United Nations Relief and Works Agency for Palestine Refugees in the Near East, was established by United Nations General Assembly resolution 302 (IV) of December 8, 1949 to carry out direct relief and works programs for Palestine refugees. The agency began operations on May 1, 1950. In the absence of a solution to the Palestine refugee problem, the General Assembly has repeatedly renewed UNRWA's mandate, most recently extending it until June 30, 2005.

Yahya Ayash

Known as the "Engineer," he is a Hamas activist who was blamed for a series of suicide bombings in Israel. Ayash was assassinated by Israel in 1996 when his booby-trapped mobile phone went off in a house in Beit Lahia, Gaza.

Zahrah school

A primary school located in the Jenin refugee camp.

Bibliography

"Adalah and LAW Call on Supreme Court to Establish Procedures for the Removal of Palestinian Bodies from Jenin Refugee Camp." *Adalah, The Legal Center for Arab Minority Rights in Israel*, April 15, 2002. August 25, 2002. <http://www.adalah.org/press_releases/02_04_15.htm>.

"ADL Says U.N. Report on Jenin 'Shouldn't Have Been Written.'" *Anti Defamation League*, August 1, 2002. August 10 2002 <http://www.adl.org/PresRele/UnitedNations_94/4140_94.asp>.

"Amnesty International Calls for Immediate International Humanitarian Assistance." *Amnesty International*, April 17 2002. August 1 2002 <http://www.amnestyusa.org/news/2002/israel04172002.html>.

"Amnesty International Calls on the UN Security Council to Immediately Deploy an Independent Investigation into Human Rights Abuses in Jenin." *Amnesty International*, April 16, 2002. August 1 2002 <http://www.amnestyusa.org/news/2002/israel04162002.html>.

Borger, Julian, Chris McGreal, and Ewen MacAskill. "Bush Says Israeli Invasion of Jenin Must Be Investigated." *Guardian Unlimited*, April 20 2002. August 15, 2002 <http://www.guardian.co.uk/israel/Story/0,2763,687669,00.html>.

Cock, Jonathan. "Where is Jamal's Body?" *Al-Ahram Weekly*, May 30, 2002. August 12, 2002 <http://www.ahram.org.eg/weekly/2002/588/re4.htm>.

Deen, Thalif. "Group Slams U.N. Report on Israeli Attack on

Jenin." *Common Dreams*, August 2, 2002. August 20, 2002 <http: //www.commondreams.org/headlines02/0802-03.htm>.

Gallagher, Mike. "Jenin Survivors Describe Israeli Operation." *Rense*, April 22, 2002. August 28, 2002 < http://www.rense.com/general24/ jenins.htm>.

"Geneva Convention Relative to the Protection of Civilian Persons in Time of War."
Office of the High Commissioner for Human Rights, May 10, 2002 <http://www.unhchr.ch/html/menu3/b/92.htm>.

Giacaman, Rita, and Penny Johnson. "Who Lives in Jenin Refugee Camp? A Brief Statistical Profile." *The Electronic Intifada*, April 14, 2002. May 12, 2002 <http://electronicintifada.net/forreference/ briefings/jenincamp.html>.

Giovanni, Janine Di. "Children Scream for Water in the 'City of Bombers'." *Times Online*, April 9, 2002. May 5 2002 <http: //www.timesonline.co.uk/article/0,,3-261573,00.html>.

HaCohen, Ran. "The UN from Qana to Jenin: Why the Secretary General's Report Cannot Be Trusted." *Antiwar.com*, August 14, 2002. August 14, 2002 <http://www.antiwar.com/hacohen/h081402.html>.

Huggler, Justin, and Phil Reeves. "Human Rights Groups Find Evidence of War Crimes in Jenin." *The Independent*, May 3, 2002. August 15, 2002 <http://news.independent.co.uk/world/middle_east/story.jsp?st ory=291385>.

Huggler, Justin, and Phil Reeves. "Once Upon a Time in Jenin." *The Independent*, April 24, 2002. August 15, 2002 <http: //news.independent.co.uk/world/middle_east/story.jsp?story=28859 2>.

"'Human Shield' Dies as Hamas Man is Killed by Troops." *Ha'aretz*, August 17, 2002. August 20, 2002 <http://www.haaretzdaily.com/ hasen/pages/ShArt.jhtml?itemNo=197810&contrassID=2&subContr

assID=1&sbSubContrassID=0&listSrc=Y>.

"Jenin Camp." UNRWA, the United Nations Relief and Works Agency, August 10, 2002 <http://www.un.org/unrwa/refugees/wb/jenin.html>.

"Israel in Charge of Position, Rejects Security Resolution 1405, Forcing Secretary-General to Disband Fact-Finding Team to Jenin Refugee Camp." Palestine and the UN, May 2002: 1-3.

Israel in Lebanon: The Report of the International Commission to Enquire into Reported Violations of International Law by Israel During its Invasion of Lebanon. London, Ithaca, 1983.

Kafala, Tarik. "What is a War Crime?" *BBC News Online*, July 3, 2001. August 1, 2002 <http://news.bbc.co.uk/1/hi/world/europe/1420133.stm>.

Khromchenko, Yulie. "Displaced Reality: Impressions from a Visit to Jenin." *CounterPunch*, May 21, 2002. August 20, 2002 <http://www.counterpunch.org/jenin0521.html>.

Kimmerling, Baruch. "The Battle of Jenin as an Inter-Ethnic War." *CounterPunch*, May 1, 2002. August 20, 2002 <http://www.counterpunch.org/kimmerling0501.html>.

Left, Sarah, and Jeffery Simon. "Middle East Timeline 2002: January to March." *Guardian Unlimited*, April 8, 2002. August 10, 2002 <http://www.guardian.co.uk/israel/Story/0,2763,630014,00.html>.

Lynfield, Ben, and Roy Macmillan. "Are the Israelis Guilty of Mass Murder?" *The Scotsman*, April 19, 2002. August 15, 2002 <http://news.scotsman.com/archive.cfm?id=417052002>.

McGowan, Daniel, and Marc H. Ellis, eds. *Remembering Deir Yassin: The Future of Israel and Palestine.* New York: Olive Branch, 1998.

McGreal, Chris, and Brian Whitaker. "Israel Accused Over Jenin Assault." *Guardian Unlimited*, April 23, 2002. August 15, 2002 <http://www.guardian.co.uk/israel/Story/0,2763,688959,00.html>.

Morris, Benny. *The Birth of the Palestinian Refugee Problem, 1947-1949.* Cambridge: Cambridge University Press, 1989.

Pank, Philip, and Jeffery Simon. "Middle East Timeline 2002: April." *Guardian Unlimited*, June 26, 2002. August 15, 2002 <http://www.guardian.co.uk/israel/Story/0,2763,684692,00.html>.

Physicians for Human Rights, *Physicians for Human Rights Forensic Team Preliminary Assessment: Jenin, April 21-23, 2002*, April 30 2002. August 1 2002 <http://www.phrusa.org/research/mneutrality/report_043002.html>.

Podur, Justine. "What Happened in Jenin? What is Happening in Jenin." *Znet*, August 2002. August 28, 2002 <http://www.zmag.org/content/showarticle.cfm?SectionID=22&ItemID=2190>.

Reeves, Phil. "Amid the Ruins of Jenin, the Grisly Evidence of a War Crime." *The Independent*, April 16 2002. August 15 2002 <http://news.independent.co.uk/world/middle_east/story.jsp?story=285413>.

Reeves, Phil, and Justine Huggler. "Nurse Shot Through the Heart and Man in Wheelchair Among Jenin Dead." *The Independent*, April 25, 2002. August 13, 2002 <http://news.independent.co.uk/world/middle_east/story.jsp?story=291385>.

Reinhart, Tanya. "Jenin: The Propaganda Battle." *CounterPunch*, April 24, 2002. May 11, 2002 <http://www.counterpunch.org/reinhart0424.html>.

Report of the Secretary-General Prepared Pursuant of General Assembly Resolution ES-10/10. 2002. United Nation. August 3, 2002 <http://www.un.org/peace/jenin>.

"Report: Peres Calls Jenin Operation 'Massacre.'" *The Jerusalem Post*, April 9, 2002. August 10, 2002 <http://www.jpost.com/Editions/2002/04/09/LatestNews/LatestNews.46578.html>.

Security Council Resolution 1405 Palestine and the UN. May 2002: 2-3.

Serious Breaches of Human Rights and Humanitarian Law. Amnesty International April 22, 2002. August 1, 2002 <http://www.amnestyusa.org/news/2002/israel04222002.html>.

Smith, Charles D. *Palestine and the Arab-Israeli Conflict.* 3rd ed. New York: St. Martin, 1996.

The Beirut Massacre: Press Profile. 2nd ed. New York: Claremont Research and Publications, 1984.

The Humanitarian Situation in the West Bank and the Gaza Strip. United Nations December 5, 2001. August 10, 2002 <http://www.un.org/unrwa/news/statements/genevasp.pdf>.

Williams, Dan. "Israeli Army Under Fire for Looting." *Reuters* August 25, 2002. August 28, 2002 <http://news.findlaw.com/international/s/20020826/mideastlootingdc.html>.

Index

Acknowledgements

The publishers and editor of this book are indebted to many individuals for their help in actualizing this project, especially to those who put their lives on the line to transport reporters to and from the Jenin refugee camp under curfew, to those who facilitated the interviews, to the scholars who shared their thoughts and experiences with us, to the journalists and internationals who visited the camp, and to all others.

Special thanks goes to Professor Noam Chomsky for his support and encouragement and for his thoughtful preface to the book, and to Jennifer Loewenstein for her photographs and support throughout the project. Thank you to all of our essayists, editors, proofreaders, photographers, and facilitators. A special thank you to Ms. Suzanne Baroud, whose excellent editing skills, vision, and thoughtful contributions have helped produce this book in the best form possible. A heartfelt thank you to Mr. Hani Arafat, the head of Al-Amwaj TV and radio station in the West Bank for his valuable contributions to this book.

The introduction of this book was based primarily on newspaper reports published prior, during, or after the invasion of Jenin. Some of the most helpful resources have been press releases from Amnesty International, Human Rights Watch, and publications such as the British *Independent*, the British *Guardian*, *Arabia.com*, *Common Dreams*, the United Nations website, the UN *Observer* and *International Report*, the *Electronic Intifada* website, the *CounterPunch* website, Egypt's *Al-Ahram Weekly*, The Report of the Secretary General on Jenin, the *Scotsman*, *BBC News*, *Ha'aretz*, *ZNet*, *Antiwar.com*, *B'Tselem*, LAW, *The History Place*, *Jerusalem Post*, and many others.

We would also like to thank many others whose valuable contributions made this volume possible. Our sincere thanks to Sufian Abdulhadi, Fathe Alwan, Julie Boulter-Buetow, Michelle Gasparek, Elizabeth Gimmestad, Christiane Martens, Ibrahim Muhanna, Maref Quran, Paul

Rafferty, Mark Schneider, and Eric Soderlund. Our sincere apologies to those whom we have mistakenly omitted. We are indebted to you all.

Special thanks to the crew in Jenin: Samira Essa Abdullah, Majda Kassem Aqil, A'yesha Kassem Aqil, Ali Samudi, Mae Ziad Shaheen, Muhammad Ibrahim Shawish, Muhammad Turkman, and Mahfouz Abu Turk.

Bios

Ali Samudi, project facilitator, is a Palestinian journalist who was born and raised in the town of Jenin in the West Bank. Samudi is a Reuters cameraman and runs Al-Majd Press, an independent press office in Jenin. His footage following the Jenin invasion was broadcast on CNN, BBC, and Al-Jazeera. Samudi was wounded by a tank shell on September 11, 2001 while filming an Israeli army incursion into Jenin. He was hospitalized for three months. Mr. Samudi is a correspondent for *Al-Quds* newspaper in Jenin. He also hosts political discussions on Jenin Central Television, an independent news station based in Jenin.

Mahfouz Abu Turk, photojournalist, is a Jerusalem-based Palestinian photographer and journalist. Abu Turk has worked with leading news agencies and publications around the world, including Agency France Press, Associated Press, and the *Washington Report.* He currently works with Reuters. Abu Turk's photographs have been exhibited in Italy, Greece, Germany, South Africa, the United States, France, and several Arab countries. Through a maze of checkpoints and a hail of bullets, he was the first journalist to enter the camp following the invasion.

Mamoun Sakkal, calligrapher, is an award-winning calligrapher, graphic designer, interior designer, and architect. Sakkal was born in Aleppo in northern Syria and is currently based in Bothell, Washington. For more: www.sakkal.com.

Suzanne Baroud, assistant editor, is the Managing Editor of *PalestineChronicle.com,* a leading online Palestinian publication. A native of Seattle, she lived and worked in the West Bank for three years. She has co-authored a short story, which was included in the anthology *Children of Israel, Children of Palestine* (Pocket Books, 1998).

Ramzy Baroud, Editor

Ramzy Baroud was born and raised in a refugee camp in the Gaza Strip and currently resides near Seattle with his wife Suzanne and two daughters. His articles have appeared in the *Washington Post,* the *Christian Science Monitor*, and the *Seattle Post-Intelligencer*, as well as numerous overseas publications. Baroud is the founder of the online magazine *PalestineChronicle.com* and his Arabic commentaries regularly appear in the London-based *al-Arab International* newspaper.

Noam Chomsky

Noam Chomsky is among America's most prominent academic dissidents. A linguistics professor at MIT, he has authored over 30 political books examining US intervention in the developing world, the political economy of human rights, and corporate media's use of propaganda. Chomsky is an astute critic of international affairs and US foreign policy. His works include: *American Power and the New Mandarins*; *Peace in the Middle East?*; *The Political Economy of Human Rights, Vol. I and II* (with E.S. Herman); *Towards a New Cold War*; *Fateful Triangle*; *Pirates and Emperors*; *The Culture of Terrorism*; *Manufacturing Consent* (with E.S. Herman); *Deterring Democracy*; *Rethinking Camelot: JFK, the Vietnam War and US Political Culture*; *World Orders, Old and New*; *Powers and Prospects*; *The Common Good*; *Profit Over People*; *The New Military Humanism*; *Rogue States*; *A New Generation Draws the Line*; *9-11*; and *Understanding Power*.